Wootto:

One Hundr   ago

The Great War

Sheridan Parsons

Part 1 of the revised and extended edition of
Wootton Bassett in the Great War (2014)

Dedicated to those who served,
those who fell,
and those who stayed at home.

*It bain't no use grousing.
What mun be, mun be.*

Contents

Illustrations

Thanks

So many people have sustained me during the writing and rewriting of this book, over over six years, that I cannot possibly name them all here. Rest assured that you are all appreciated. My particular thanks go to the families of those in the book, who have generously contributed their memories, letters, diaries and photographs; the staff at Swindon Library's local history team, Katherine Cole, Darryl Moody, and Jon Ratcliffe, who were wonderful gatekeepers fabulous company during the hours I spent trawling through the library's resources; everyone I have consulted at local museums, archives, history societies, and regimental museums, particularly Claire Skinner and Terry Bracher at the Wiltshire and Swindon History Centre; the volunteers at Wootton Bassett Town Hall Museum; everyone at The Rifles Berkshire and Wiltshire Museum; Mark Sutton from Swindon, and Bob Lloyd from Purton, whose passion and dedication to the soldiers of Wiltshire is utterly magnificent; the members of the 'Swindon in the Great War' team (now disbanded); Frances Bevan, an irrepressible historian with a boundless knowledge of Swindon; Sandra Gittins, an inspiring researcher of the Great Western Railways; and the Swindon Advertiser and the Wiltshire Gazette and Herald, for allowing me to quote liberally from their pages.

I would like to pay tribute to D-Day veteran Ken Scott, who died in 2015. His respect for the "old boys" of the Great War, the memories he shared with me, and his unstinting appreciation of all those who served were instrumental in my decision to develop a brief memorial to the fallen into the complete story of Wootton Bassett's war. Handing a copy of my book to him and having him tell me how much he was enjoying it were sources of great pride to me.

Thanks

Since publishing Wootton Bassett in the Great War in 2014, I have gained valuable experience as an archive assistant under the exacting tutelage of Matthew McMurray, archivist at the Royal Voluntary Services Archives. My academic skills have been vastly improved by undertaking a Master's degree in Local and Family History at Dundee University, during which I have been greatly inspired by all my tutors and fellow-students, especially archivist and historian Dr Caroline Shenton. My achievements at Dundee have permitted me to join the Register of Qualified Genealogists.

I would like to thank my family and friends for their support; my first edition proofreaders, Sam Burgess, a warm and enthusiastic librarian (the best kind), and Angie Reeves, whose honesty and insight make her a wonderful friend and ally; Hazel Newson for her heart-warming efforts on behalf of our town; Jack Wilson, a young man whose enthusiasm reminded me that history is not just of interest to older folk, and that his generation will become our own storytellers; the Wiltshire Golf and Leisure Club for the hours I spent typing in their bar; my valued associates on Twitter and Instagram; and the fabulous wider community of genealogists.

As always, I offer my adoration and thanks to my wonderful husband Mike, for his constant patience, tolerance, and encouragement during the thousands of hours I have spent studying, writing, and researching, rather than paying attention to the housework, or indeed to him. I could not have achieved my original book, or this, its successor, without his amazing love and support.

Resources

I have consulted a wide range of resources during the writing of this book. If I were able to turn back the clock and start again from scratch, I would footnote everything. Sadly it is too late to rectify this glaring omission, so I offer my sincere apologies for any omissions and offer the briefest of summaries here.

Principal sources to which I have referred frequently include: the Wiltshire Gazette and Herald; the Swindon Advertiser; numerous official records including 'Soldiers Died in the Great War' (a list of those who died, published by His Majesty's Stationery Office in 1921), military service records, medal roll cards, soldier's effects records, census records, and many more. These were mainly accessed via Ancestry, Find My Past, and the National Archives. I have also made good use of the superb digitised records of the Commonwealth War Graves Commission, and I am particularly proud of being able to contribute a few small corrections to their records and memorials.

A considerable effort has been made to improve this edition by cross-referencing every single Wootton Bassett name and address with the 1918 electoral roll, held at the Wiltshire and Swindon History Centre. I have also added information about local men and women who trained as nurses. In this edition, I have also made more use of war diaries, which were produced by individual battalions during the war. They rarely include the names of individuals, but nearly always provide valuable insight into the battalion's activities, and context for the experience and loss of the fallen. On a lighter note, I have included lots of information about residents' cars and motorcycles. I have also made frequent use of General Register Office Records (if only I had the funds to buy more certificates!) and the valuable cemetery records made available online, and indexed by Royal Wootton Bassett Town

Council. Other useful sources have included 'Wootton Bassett' by P J Gingell; the Wiltshire Family History Society's records; the Town Council's 1914 House Numbering Survey; 'Swindon's War Record' by W D Bavin; the Victoria County History of Wiltshire; the Wootton Bassett YMCA yearbooks of 1919 and 1913, courtesy of the Cadbury Research Library; photographs from Swindon Museum and Art Gallery; wartime issues of the Wootton Bassett Parish Magazine; old issues of the Wiltshire Archaeological Society Magazine; Kelly's Directories; the Great Western Railway magazines; Library and Archives Canada; the National Archives of Australia; and the British Newspaper Archive; 'Early Motor Vehicle Registration in Wiltshire' edited by Ian Hicks.

I owe a great debt of gratitude to the descendants and families who have shared their information and photographs. I am also indebted to Ancestry for the facility to contact living relatives.

Town Map

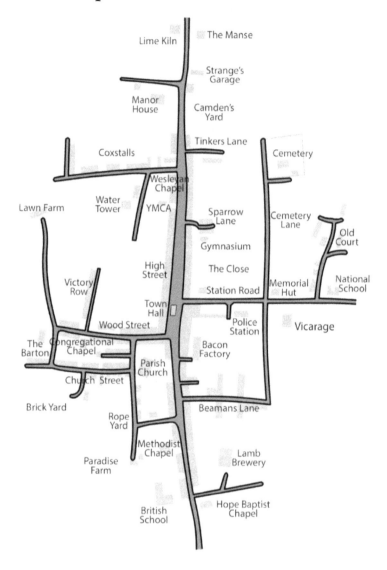

Wootton Bassett in the Great War
Town Centre Map
Sheridan Parsons © 2014

[v]

Country Map

Hay Lane

To Swindon

Bolingbroke
Arms

Lydiard
Park

Mannington

Toothill

Hook Farm

Railway

Hook War
Memorial

Hook
School

Creeches
Farm

M4 opened 1971

Midge Hall

Spittleborough

Church
Hills

Flaxlands

Coped
Hall

Ryelands

Wickfield
Farm

Hay Lane   Canal

Ballards
Ash

Longleaze

Upper
Woodshaw

Highgate
Farm

Horsell's
Lake

Stoneover
Lane

Lower
Woodshaw

Chaddington

Vowley

Salthrop

Basset
Down

Folly
Wood

Spratts
Barn

Nore
Marsh

Park
Grounds

Brynards
Hill

Bincknoll
Lane

Callow
Hill

Lawn
Farm

High
Street

Brewery

War
Memorial

Dairy

Gas
Works

School
Hill

Railway

New
Road

Station

Dunnington

Marlborough Road

Whitehill
Farm

Skew
Bridge

Cotmarsh

Whitehill Lane

Canal

Knights
Farm

Hunt
Mill

Grittenham

Greenhill
Common

Old Park

Hunt
Mill
Farm

Lower
Greenhill

Railway

Hart
Farm

Vastern
Wharf

Little
Park

Vastern
Manor

Vastern
Manor
Farm

Upper
Greenhill

Breach
Lane

Canal

Tockenham
Wick

Black
Dog

Tockenham
Corner War
Memorial

Tockenham
Greenway

Wootton Bassett in the Great War
Farms, Hamlets and Villages
(not to scale)
Sheridan Parsons © 2014

[vi]

Key to Roll of Honour

The following pages list the names and details of the fallen in alphabetical order within each area. The men are listed as follows:

Area. This is the most significant local area where it is appropriate for the man to be remembered. For this Roll of Honour, a War Memorial inscription is taken to be more significant than a paper trail. The lack of an inscription should never be construed to mean that the man (or his next of kin) did not live in that area. There may be many reasons why he does not appear on a formal memorial.

Name and gallantry awards

Rank and regiment at the time of death

Cause of death - date of death - age at death

Burial information or Memorial to the Missing

Last known local address. This is most often the man's address at the time of his death, but may be a former address, or the address of his next of kin, if he was not registered in the local area at that time.

War Memorial. A paper Roll of Honour is only listed here if it is the most significant existing Memorial. 'No known War Memorial' generally refers to local memorials which I have researched fully, but in some cases, broader searches have been undertaken.

Full stories and additional details can be found in the relevant Town and Country volumes of this book. A handful of men whose biographies are included in these books are not listed in this Roll of Honour. This is because they have some significance to the story being told, but they (or their next of kin) never lived in the area.

Roll of Honour
Wootton Bassett

Gilbert Angelinetta
Rifleman, 7th Kings Rifles
Killed in Action 30 Jul 1915 age 20
No Known Grave - Menin Gate Memorial
47 Church Street
Wootton Bassett War Memorial

Oliver Ernest Angelinetta
Private, 6th Wiltshire Regiment
Killed in Action 8 Jul 1916 age 19
Buried at Serre Road No.2 Cemetery
120 High Street
Wootton Bassett War Memorial

Lionel Arthur Ashfield DFC
Lieutenant, Royal Air Force
Killed in Action 16 Jul 1918, age 19
Buried at Ramscappelle Road Military Cemetery
The Manor House, High Street
Born in Wootton Bassett

Wootton Bassett

Arthur Beazley
Lance Corporal, 7th King's Shropshire Light Infantry
Died of wounds 30 Mar 1918 age 31
Buried at Cabaret Rouge British Cemetery
16 Wood Street
Wootton Bassett War Memorial

Herbert Beazley
Rifleman, Post Office Rifles
Died of wounds 17 Jul 1918 age 18
Buried at Franvillers Communal Cemetery & Extension
16 Wood Street
Wootton Bassett War Memorial

Christopher Blanchett
Sergeant, 9th Canadian
Killed in Action 17 Jun 1915 age 33
No Known Grave - Vimy Memorial
13 Victory Row
Wootton Bassett War Memorial

Godfrey Arthur William Ephraim Bridgeman
Private, 2nd Wiltshire Regiment
Killed in Action 18 Oct 1916 age 35
Buried at Warlencourt British Cemetery
Nore Marsh Farm
Christian Malford War Memorial

Wootton Bassett

Alan Brown
Private, 8th Somerset Light Infantry
Killed in Action 10 Jul 1918 age 19
Buried at Couin New British Cemetery
Cross Keys, 136 High Street
Wootton Bassett War Memorial

Eltham Brian Brown
Private, Royal Marines Light Infantry
Killed in Action 26 Oct 1917 age 23
No Known Grave - Tyne Cot Memorial
Cross Keys, 136 High Street
Wootton Bassett War Memorial

Hedley Brown
1st Class Stoker, Royal Navy
Killed in Action 22 Sep 1914 age 22
At Sea - Chatham War Memorial
Cross Keys, 136 High Street
Wootton Bassett War Memorial

Reginald Herbert Buckland
Private, 6th Wiltshire Regiment
Killed in action 2 Jul 1916 age 20
No Known Grave - Thiepval Memorial
Church Street
No known War Memorial

Reginald Buckland
Private, 1st Wiltshire Regiment
Died of wounds 8 Nov 1918 age 31
Buried at Mont Huon Military Cemetery
The Barton
No known War Memorial

William Eli Burchell
Private, 2nd Wiltshire Regiment
Killed in action 15 Jun 1915 age 35
No Known Grave - Le Touret Memorial
Hunt Mill Road
Wootton Bassett War Memorial

Herbert Jeffrey Chequer
Gunner, 172nd Siege Battery
Drowned 31 Dec 1917 age 28
Buried (body recovered) - Alexandria Hadra War Memorial
109 High Street
GWR Carriage and Paint Shop Memorial

James Clarke
Sergeant, 1st Dorsets Regiment
Died of illness 29 Jan 1917 age 36
Buried at Durrington Cemetery
Wootton Bassett
No known War Memorial

Ernest Sidney Cox
Private, 16th Australian
Killed in Action   29 Apr 1915 age 21
No Known Grave - Lone Pine Memorial
Rylands Farm, Swindon Road
Wootton Bassett War Memorial

Sydney Harold Curry
Cooper's Crew, Royal Navy
Killed in Action 12 Aug 1915 age 17
At Sea - Plymouth Naval Memorial
56 Station Road
No known War Memorial

Henry Philip Drury
Private, 1st Wiltshire Regiment
Killed in Action 20 Sep 1914 age 29
No Known Grave - La Ferté-sous-Jouarre Memorial
Spratts Barn Farm
No known War Memorial

Albert Edmonds
Air Mechanic 2nd Class, Royal Flying Corps
Air Accident 20 Aug 1917 age 30
Buried at Wootton Bassett Cemetery
Laurel Villa, Coped Hall
Wootton Bassett War Memorial

Wootton Bassett

Sydney Fisher Foster
Private, 20th RGA
Died (probably of illness) 4 Nov 1918 age 21
Buried at Alexandria Hadra War Memorial Cemetery
St Helens, 116 High Street
Wootton Bassett War Memorial

Leonard Franklin
Private, 13th Welch
Killed in Action 18 Sep 1918 age 38
No Known Grave - Vis-en-Artois Memorial
Probably born in Beamans Lane
No known War Memorial

Henry James Gibbs
Lance Corporal, 1st Wiltshire Regiment
Killed in Action 8 Jul 1916 age 29
No Known Grave - Thiepval Memorial
Beamans Lane
Wootton Bassett War Memorial

John Charles Bromwich Gibbs
Private, 1st Wiltshire Regiment
Died of wounds 10 Feb 1917 age 19
Buried at Bailleul Communal Cemetery Extension Nord
30 Station Road
Wootton Bassett War Memorial

Thomas Edward Gibson
Acting Lance Corporal, 526th Field Coy Royal Engineers
Killed in Action 21 Apr 1918 age 26
Buried at Chocques Military Cemetery
The Angel, 47 High Street
Wootton Bassett War Memorial

Francis Whicher Greenaway
Sapper, 126th Field Co Royal Engineers
Died of wounds 4 May 1916 age 26
Buried at La Neuville Communal Cemetery
1 Victory Row
Heathfield War Memorial, St Philip's Memorial, Burwash Common,
Heathfield Oddfellows Roll of Honour.

Frederick Stanley Haines
Corporal, 4th Seaforth Highlanders
Died of wounds 19 Oct 1916 age 24
Buried at Purton St Mary's
Clarendon House, 37 High Street
Purton War Memorial

Walter Thomas Ewart Harris
Private, 7th Wiltshire Regiment
Died of wounds 13 Nov 1920 age 22
Buried at Wootton Bassett Cemetery
46 High Street
Wootton Bassett War Memorial

Wootton Bassett

Samuel Gordon Hart
Sergeant, 54th RFA
Died of wounds 26 May 1917 age 20
Buried at Struma Military Cemetery
Crown Hotel, 131 High Street
Wootton Bassett War Memorial

Edwin Helps
Rifleman, Post Office Rifles
Killed in Action 15 Dec 1916 age 37
Buried at Woods Cemetery
Burmah Villa, 8 Coxstalls
Wootton Bassett War Memorial

Albert Edward Hewer
Private, 1st Gloucestershire Regiment
Killed in Action 23 Dec 1914 age 33
No Known Grave - Le Touret Memorial
39 Church Street
Wootton Bassett War Memorial

John Hird
Private, 2nd King's Own Royal Lancaster Regiment
Killed in Action 8 May 1915 age 30
No Known Grave - Menin Gate Memorial
18 Church Street
Wootton Bassett War Memorial

Wootton Bassett

Charles Henry Hughes
Private, 7th Gloucestershire Regiment
Died 4 Aug 1916 age 26
No Known Grave - Basra War Memorial
41 Church Street
Wootton Bassett War Memorial

Alfred Reginald Hunt
Gunner, 1st/1st Essex RGA
Died of wounds 22 Dec 1917 age 23
Buried at Mendinghem Military Cemetery
1 Victory Row
Wootton Bassett War Memorial

Archibald Harry Hunt
Private, 21st Australian
Killed in Action 28 Jul 1916 age 30
Buried at Becourt Military Cemetery
Hurstead House, 107 High Street
Wootton Bassett War Memorial

George Seymour Hunt
Private, 2nd Wiltshire Regiment
Died of wounds 3 May 1917 age 26
Buried at Abbeville Communal Cemetery Extension
Hurstead House, 107 High Street
Wootton Bassett War Memorial

Harry John Hunt
Private, 2nd Wiltshire Regiment
Died of Wounds 8 Jul 1916 age 34
No Known Grave - Thiepval Memorial
14 Victory Row
Wootton Bassett War Memorial

Joseph Clarence Hunt
Private, 2nd Wiltshire Regiment
Died of Wounds   23 Jul 1916 age 19
Buried at La Neuville British Cemetery
1 Victory Row
Wootton Bassett War Memorial

Lionel Frederick Job Hunt, MM
Private, 21st Northumberlands
Killed in Action 10 Sep 1917 age 19
No Known Grave - Thiepval Memorial
5 Sparrow Lane
Wootton Bassett War Memorial

Reginald Hunt
Private, 2nd Wiltshire Regiment
Killed in Action 12 Mar 1915 age 20
No Known Grave - Le Touret Memorial
3 Old Court
Wootton Bassett War Memorial

Wootton Bassett

Henry John Huxley
Colour Acting Sergeant, Army Veterinary Corps
Died of wounds 22 Aug 1918 age 35
Buried at Terlincthun British Cemetery
174 High Street
No known War Memorial

William Jacobs
Private, 1st Wiltshire Regiment
Killed in Action 12 Apr 1918 age 19
No Known Grave - Ploegsteert Memorial
Born in Old Court
Born in Wootton Bassett

Leslie, Ernest Hodgson
Captain, 47th West Ontario Canadian
Died of Illness 16 Mar 1919 age 34
Buried at St Thomas, Stockton Heath
Born in Wootton Bassett
No known War Memorial

Charles Henry Lovelock
Private, 5th Wiltshire Regiment
Died of wounds   28 Jan 1917 age 22
Buried at Amara War Cemetery
Woodshaw Cottages (near Garraways)
Wootton Bassett War Memorial

George Edward Lovelock
Private, 2nd Wiltshire Regiment
Killed in Action 18 Oct 1916 age 23
No Known Grave - Thiepval Memorial
Woodshaw Cottages (near Garraways)
Wootton Bassett War Memorial

Alfred Harry Marsh
Private, 2nd Royal Sussex Regiment
Killed in Action 30 Oct 1914 age 31
No Known Grave - Menin Gate Memorial
Beaufort Brewery employee
No known War Memorial

Sidney Albert Merrett, DCM
Corporal, 2nd Wiltshire Regiment
Killed in Action 9 Apr 1917 age 29
Buried at Neuville-Vitasse Cemetery
172 High Street
Wootton Bassett War Memorial

Henry James Merritt
Lance Corporal, 5th Wiltshire Regiment
Drowned 15 Apr 1917 age 31
Buried At Sea - Chatby Memorial
172 High Street
Wootton Bassett War Memorial

Wootton Bassett

George Moulding
Sergeant, 1st Wiltshire Regiment
Died of wounds 25 Mar 1918 age 32
Buried at Puchevillers British Cemetery
Church Street
St Lawrence's Church War Memorial plaque, Lechlade

Charles Robert Ogburn
Private, 3rd Ox and Bucks Light Infantry
Died 26 Apr 1916 age 37
Buried at Portdown Christ Church Military Cemetery
Wood Street
No known War Memorial

Raymond Charles Painter
Private, 13th Essex Regiment
Killed in Action 27 Jun 1917 age 25
Buried at Gorre British and Indian Cemetery
27 Coxstalls
Wootton Bassett War Memorial

Albert James Peaple
Private, 1st Wiltshire Regiment
Killed in Action 31 Oct 1914 age 29
No Known Grave - Le Touret Memorial
Woodshaw Cottages (near Garraways)
Wootton Bassett War Memorial

Rupert Charles Rowe
Company Sergeant Major, 5th Wiltshire Regiment
Killed in Action 21 Jan 1917 age 32
Buried at Amara War Cemetery
High Street
Wootton Bassett War Memorial

William James Sainsbury
Private, 15th Royal Warwickshire Regiment
Killed in Action 14 Apr 1918 age 34
Buried at Morbecque British Cemetery
12 Victory Row
Wootton Bassett War Memorial

Augustus Montague Sargent
Second Lieutenant, 15th Sherwood Foresters
Died of wounds 27 Apr 1918 age 34
Buried at Doullens Communal Cemetery Extension No 1
Manor Villa, 75 High Street
Wootton Bassett War Memorial

George Francis Sawyer
Private, 1st Wiltshire Regiment
Killed in Action 13 Oct 1914 age 30
No Known Grave - Le Touret Memorial
The Lodge, Hay Lane
Wootton Bassett War Memorial and Hay Lane Roll of Honour

William Sly
Sergeant, 2nd Wiltshire Regiment
Killed in Action 8 Jul 1916 age 29
No Known Grave - Thiepval Memorial
18 Wood Street
St Giles War Memorial, Lea

Hubert Harry Styles Street, MM
Lance Corporal, MM, 57th Australian
Killed in Action 5 Mar 1918 age 31
Buried at La Plus Douve Farm Cemetery
155 High Street
Wootton Bassett War Memorial

Harold Lyttleton George Tayler
Private, 8th Winnipeg Rifles, Canadian Exp Force
Killed in Action 10 Nov 1917 age 22
No Known Grave - Menin Gate Memorial
The Angel, 47 High Street
Wootton Bassett War Memorial

Arthur Sidney Twine
Private, 6th Wilts Regiment
Killed in Action 2 Jul 1916 age 22
No Known Grave - Thiepval Memorial
2 The Barton
Wootton Bassett War Memorial

Arthur Twine
Private, 6th Wiltshire Regiment
Killed in Action 5 Jun 1917 age 35
No Known Grave - Menin Gate Memorial
64 Church Street
Wootton Bassett War Memorial

William Howard Twine
2nd Lieutenant (Temp), 2nd York and Lancs Regiment
Killed in Action 13 May 1916 age 26
Buried at Essex Farm Cemetery
Greenhill Common Farm
Wootton Bassett War Memorial

William Charles Watson
Cook's Mate, Royal Navy
Drowned 31 May 1916 age 22
Buried At Sea - Portsmouth Naval Memorial
Bradenstoke
Portsmouth Naval Memorial

Frank Watts
Lance Corporal, 8th Royal Fusiliers
Killed in Action 19 Jul 1917 age 27
No Known Grave - Arras Memorial
1 Church Street
Wootton Bassett War Memorial

William Albert Westmacott
Air Mechanic 2nd Class, Royal Air Force
Died of Pneumonia 9 Mar 1919 age 24
Buried at Wootton Bassett Cemetery
Upper Greenhill (father at 173 High Street)
Wootton Bassett War Memorial

Wright, Edgar James
Sergeant, Army Veterinary Corps
Died due to illness 26 Jun 1915 age 32
Buried at Wootton Bassett Cemetery
13 High Street
Wootton Bassett War Memorial

Roll of Honour
Lydiard Tregoze and Marlborough Road

Charles Barnes
Private, 5th Wiltshire Regiment
Killed in Action 18 Oct 1915 age 19
Buried at Green Hill Cemetery, Suvla
Born in Wootton Bassett, later lived in Hook
Hook War Memorial

Francis Charles Clark
Private, 5th Wiltshire Regiment
Died of wounds 13 Apr 1916 age 18
Buried - Amara War Cemetery
Born in Downend, Gloucestershire, later lived in Wickfield Lane
No known War Memorial

William George Clifford
Private, 1st Wiltshire Regiment
Died of wounds 19 Jan 1915 age 35
Buried at Netley, Hampshire
Born in Clevancy, later lived in The Lodge, Hay Lane
Hay Lane Roll of Honour

Lydiard Tregoze and Marlborough Road

John Comley
Private, 5th Wiltshire Regiment
Killed in Action 10 Aug 1915 age 37
No Known Grave - Helles Memorial
Studley Grange, Hay Lane
No known War Memorial

William James Dixon
Private, 2nd Wiltshire Regiment
Killed in Action 17 Oct 1916
No Known Grave - Thiepval Memorial
Lived in Thornhill
No known War Memorial

Philip Charles Drury
Gunner, 86th ABAC RFA
Killed in Action 30 Sep 1917 age 23
Buried at The Huts Cemetery
Born in Lydiard Tregoze, lived in Hook
GWR Roll of Honour

Arthur Robert Leonard Eacott
Private, 1st Wiltshire Regiment
Died 6 May 1918 age 33
Buried in Wootton Bassett Cemetery
Padbrook Farm, Chaddington
No War Memorial

Lydiard Tregoze and Marlborough Road

Edward David Embling
Private, 5th Wiltshire Regiment
Died of Fever 11 Sep 1916 age 26
Buried at Basra War Cemetery
Born at Spittleborough
Hook War Memorial

William John Thomas Fullaway
Private, 6th Royal Munsters
Killed in Action 1 Sep 1915 age 22
No Known Grave - Helles Memorial
Born in Rodbourne, lived at Mannington Cottages
Swindon War Memorial Tablet

Stanley Albert Hiscocks
Private, 1st Wiltshire Regiment
Killed in Action 2 Sep 1915 age 19
No Known Grave - Menin Gate Memorial
Born Thorneford, Dorset, lived at Lydiard Park
Possibly the Stanley Hiscock named on Broad Hinton War Memorial

Maurice Hitchcock
Private, 1st Gloucestershire Regiment
Died of wounds 25 Aug 1916 age 19
Buried at St Sever Cemetery
Hook
No known War Memorial

Lydiard Tregoze and Marlborough Road

Thomas George Hunt
Private, 126th Peel Canadian Expeditionary Force
Killed in Action 11 Nov 1917 age 31
Buried at Passchendaele New British Cemetery
Church Hill, Swindon Road
Toronto Old City Hall

Jesse Lawrence
Private, 6th Royal Munsters
Died of wounds 16 Aug 1915 age 29
Buried at Sea - Helles Memorial
Hook
Hook War Memorial

Victor Rowland Lovelock
Private, 2nd Wiltshire Regiment
Killed in Action 8 May 1918 age 20
No Known Grave - Tyne Cot Memorial
Hay Lane area
Hay Lane Roll of Honour, Purton War Memorial (parents' home)

Albert John Manners
Gunner 249th Siege Battery RGA
Killed in Action 29 May 1918 age 24
Buried at Brandhoek New Military Cemetery No 3
Cotmarsh Farm, Marlborough Road
Remembered on his parents' grave in Wootton Bassett Cemetery

Lydiard Tregoze and Marlborough Road

Reuben Victor Newman
Private, 2nd Warwickshire Regiment
Killed in Action 3 Sep 1916 age 19
No Known Grave - Thiepval Memorial
Hook
Hook War Memorial

Alfred James Noon
Lance Corporal, 1107th RFA
Killed in Action 24 Apr 1917 age 23
Buried at Doiran Military Cemetery
Basset Down
St Mary's Memorial Book

Wilfred John Parrott (served as William)
Private, 57th Machine Gun Corps
Died 22 Feb 1919 age 24
Buried at Duisans British Cemetery
Hook
Hook War Memorial

Henry Frank Porter
Private, 2nd Wiltshire Regiment
Killed in Action 15 Jun 1915 age 17
Buried at Cabaret Rouge British Cemetery
Lower Salthrop
Hook War Memorial

Lydiard Tregoze and Marlborough Road

Frank Shepherd
Trooper, 9th Lancers
Killed in Action 18 Jun 1917 age 30
Buried at Bully-Grenay Communal Cemetery
Basset Down
Harbledown War Memorial

Reginald Henry George Skull, MM, DCM
Private, 2nd Wiltshire Regiment
Killed in Action 9 Apr 1917 age 20
Buried at Neuville-Vitasse Road Cemetery
Hook
Hook War Memorial

Percival Harry Smart (Edge)
Private, 2nd Wiltshire Regiment
Killed in Action 12 Mar 1915 age 41
No Known Grave - Menin Gate Memorial
Hook
Hook War Memorial

John Thomas Titcombe
Private, 6th Royal Munsters
Died of wounds 17 Aug 1915 age 23
At Sea - Helles Memorial
Hook
Hook War Memorial and Swindon War Memorial

William Titcombe
Private, 1/7th Durham Light Infantry
Killed in Action 28 Mar 1918 age 24
No Known Grave - Pozieres Memorial
Hook
Swindon War Memorial

Ernest Arthur Townsend
Acting Sergeant, 2nd Wiltshire Regiment
Killed in Action 12 Mar 1915 age 27
No Known Grave - Le Touret Memorial
Toothill Cottages
Hook War Memorial

Frank Curtis Webb
Private, 11th Leicestershire Regiment
Killed in Action 21 Mar 1918 age 24
No Known Grave - Arras Memorial
Chaddington Farm
Hook War Memorial

Roll of Honour
Tockenham and Hunts Mill

William Henry Bint
Lance Corporal, 2nd Wiltshire Regiment
Died of wounds 2 Jan 1915 age 20
Buried   Kortrijk Communal Cemetery
Mermaid, Bushton
No known War Memorial

Albert Edward Church
Private, 5th Cameronians
Killed in action 29 Oct 1916 age 33
No Known Grave - Thiepval Memorial
Born in Bushton, lived in Greenway
Tockenham War Memorial

Harry Church
Private, 2nd Wiltshire Regiment
Killed in Action 9 Apr 1917 age 20
Buried at Wancourt British Cemetery
Greenway
Tockenham War Memorial

Tockenham and Hunts Mill

Percy Henry Hardiman Church
Private, 1st/5th Yorkshire Regiment
Killed in action 28 Apr 1915 age 20
No Known Grave - Menin Gate Memorial
Greenway
Tockenham War Memorial

Herbert William Fry
Private, 94th Training Reserve
Died 30 Mar 1917 age 18
Buried at St Giles, Tockenham
Tockenham
Tockenham War Memorial

George Henry Lewin Gingell
Lance Corporal 1st Wiltshire Regiment
Killed in Action 7 Jul 1916 age 31
No Known Grave - Thiepval Memorial
Tockenham
No known War Memorial

George Gingell
Able Seaman, Royal Navy
Drowned 12 Jan 1918 age 18
Buried At Sea - Portsmouth Naval Memorial
Preston
Portsmouth Naval Memorial and Windwick Bay Memorial

Tockenham and Hunts Mill

William Gingell
Private, 2nd Wiltshire Regiment
Killed in Action 27 Sep 1915 age 20
No Known Grave - Loos Memorial
Preston
Lyneham Roll of Honour Plaque

Hunt, J
Date and Details Unknown
Tockenham War Memorial

Frank Humphries
Private, 2nd Wiltshire Regiment
Killed in Action 12 Mar 1915 age 19
No Known Grave - Le Touret Memorial
Little Park Cottages
No known War Memorial

Luke Pincott
Private, Royal Army Service Corps
Died of illness 20 Apr 1919 age 30
Buried at Cologne Southern Cemetery
Hunt Mill Road
No known War Memorial

Tockenham and Hunts Mill

Lewis Herbert Reeves
Lance Sergeant, 1st Berkshire Regiment
Killed in Action 27 Jul 1916 age 23
No Known Grave - Thiepval Memorial
Tockenham
No known War Memorial

John Pickett Spackman
Guardsman, 4th Grenadier Guards
Killed by aerial bombing whilst a POW 1 Jun 1918 age 30
Buried at Anzac Cemetery, Sailly sur la Lys
Tockenham
No known War Memorial

Jasper Wilfred Walker
Private, 2nd Wiltshire Regiment
Killed in Action 21 Mar 1918 age 19
No Known Grave - Pozieres Memorial
Tockenham
Tockenham War Memorial

Eli White
Lance Corporal, 1st Wiltshire Regiment
Killed in Action 16 Sep 1914 age 27
No Known Grave - La Ferté-sous-Jouarre Memorial
Tockenham
Tockenham War Memorial (E White also served)

Roll of Honour
Brinkworth and Grittenham

Bailey, Frederick Thomas
Corporal, 10th Battalion Tank Corps
Killed in action 25 Aug 1918 age 30
Buried at Grevillers British Cemetery
Brinkworth
No known War Memorial

Phillip Carter
Private, 1st Wiltshire Regiment
Died of wounds 8 Jul 1916 age 31
Buried at Puchevillers British Cemetery
Callow Hill
Brinkworth War Memorial

Absolom Cutts
Corporal, 30th Company Machine Gun Corps
21 Mar 1918 age 22
No known grave - Pozieres Memorial
Braydonside
Brinkworth War Memorial

Brinkworth and Grittenham

William John Dixon
Private, 1st Wiltshire Regiment
Killed in Action 21 Mar 1915 age 30
Buried at La Laiterie Military Cemetery
Grittenham
East Grafton War Memorial

David Edwards
Private, 2nd Wiltshire Regiment
Killed in action 16 May 1915
No known grave - Le Touret Memorial
Brinkworth
Brinkworth War Memorial

Eggleton, Henry James Pitt, MM
Guardsman, Grenadier Guards
Died 5 Nov 1918 age 20
Buried in Brinkworth Cemetery
Glitchbury, Brinkworth
Brinkworth War Memorial

Ernest Victor Fry
Private, 2nd Wiltshire Regiment
Killed in action 21 Mar 1918 age 26
No known grave - Pozieres Memorial
Bellamy's Farm, Brinkworth
Brinkworth War Memorial

Brinkworth and Grittenham

Christopher Hinton
Private, 1st/5th Battalion Duke of Cornwall's Light Infantry
Killed in action 17 Apr 1918 age 19
No known grave - Loos Memorial
Grittenham
Brinkworth War Memorial

Edward Hunt
Private, 1st Wiltshire Regiment
Killed in action 24 Mar 1918 age 20
No known grave - Arras Memorial
Seven Locks, near Grittenham
Brinkworth War Memorial

Harry Hunt
Private, 6th Wiltshire Regiment
Killed in action 18 Feb 1916
Buried at Rue-du-Bacquerot No.1 Military Cemetery
Brinkworth
Brinkworth War Memorial

William Henry James
Private, 6th Wiltshire Regiment
Killed in action 2 Jul 1916 age 20
No known grave - Thiepval Memorial.
South View, Brinkworth
No known War Memorial

Brinkworth and Grittenham

Robert John Kibble
Private, 8th Somerset Light Infantry
Died of wounds 24 Jul 1917
Buried at Etaples Military Cemetery
Sunday Hill, Brinkworth
Brinkworth War Memorial

Horace Victor Kinch
Private, 1st Worcestershire Regiment
Killed in action 6 Jun 1918 age 19
Buried at Sissone British Cemetery
Windmill Farm, Brinkworth
No known War Memorial

Alfred Walter Manners Mapson
Private, 2nd Wiltshire Regiment, A Company
Died of wounds 5 Aug 1915 age 21
Buried in Brinkworth Cemetery
Callow Hill
Brinkworth War Memorial

James Benjamin Mapson
Private, 5th Wiltshire Regiment
5 Apr 1916 age 27
No known grave - Basra Memorial
Callow Hill
Brinkworth War Memorial

Brinkworth and Grittenham

Sidney Ernest Mapson
Private, 2nd Wiltshire Regiment A Company
Killed in action 25 Sep 1915 age 24
No known grave - Loos Memorial.
Callow Hill
Brinkworth War Memorial

Elton John Ody
Lance Corporal, 1st Wiltshire Regiment
Killed in Action 10 Apr 1918 age 19
No Known Grave - Ploegsteert Memorial
Callow Hill
Brinkworth War Memorial

Frank Theophilus Rebbeck Reynolds
Private, 1st/4th Wiltshire Regiment
Died of wounds 14 Nov 1917 age 19
Buried at Deir El Belah War Cemetery
Manor Farm Cottage, Grittenham
Brinkworth War Memorial

Tom Sellwood
Private, Wellington Regiment, New Zealand Exp Force
8 Jul 1918 age 30
Buried in Brinkworth Cemetery
Brinkworth
No known War Memorial

Brinkworth and Grittenham

Lemuel Sly
Private, 1st Wiltshire Regiment
Died of wounds 30 Oct 1914 age 21
Buried at Bethune Cemetery
Brinkworth
No known War Memorial

Charles James Smith
Corporal, 2nd Battalion Wiltshire Regiment
Killed in action 26 Sep 1915 age 37
No known grave Loos Memorial
Brinkworth
No known War Memorial

Thomas Stratton Stephens
Private, 2nd Battalion Wiltshire Regiment
Killed in action 15 Jun 1915
No known grave - Le Touret Memorial
Causeway End, Brinkworth
Brinkworth War Memorial

Fred Tanner
Private, 1st Wiltshire Regiment
Killed in action 6 Jul 1916 age 24
No known grave - Thiepval Memorial Brinkworth
Callow Hill
Brinkworth War Memorial

Brinkworth and Grittenham

Albert Edward William Vines
Serjeant, Royal Army Service Corps
Died of sickness 3 Feb 1920 age 24
Buried at Les Baraques Military Cemetery
The Street, Brinkworth
Brinkworth War Memorial

Ernest Vines
Private, 1st Battalion Wiltshire Regiment
Killed in action 10 Oct 1916
Buried at Aveluy Communal Cemetery Extension
The Street, Brinkworth
Brinkworth War Memorial

Frank Charles Vines
Private, 7th Battalion Royal West Kent Regiment
Killed in action 28 Mar 1918 age 29
No Known Grave - Pozieres Memorial
Weeks Farm, Brinkworth
Brinkworth War Memorial

Sydney Vines
Private, 1st Battalion Wiltshire Regiment
Died 31 Jan 1916
Buried at Outtersteene Communal Cemetery Extension
The Street, Brinkworth
Brinkworth War Memorial

Brinkworth and Grittenham

Reginald Percy Wheeler
Private, 45th Company Machine Gun Corps
Killed in action 25 Apr 1917 age 24
No known grave - Arras Memorial
Crossroads, Brinkworth
Brinkworth War Memorial

Wootton Bassett One Hundred Years Ago

In some ways, Wootton Bassett was a very different place in 1914 and in others much the same. It was a busy little market town, with a population just short of two thousand, dominated by the activities of the Dairy Supply Company, the Bacon Factory, a very active religious community, and regular cattle markets. By now the locals were proudly referring to Wootton Bassett as a town, no longer a village, but just as today, there was some gentle controversy over whether the name should be abbreviated to Wootton or Bassett. A talk by William Gough of Nore Marsh to the visiting Swindon Workers Educational Association made much of the local preference for "Bassett" but expressed his personal preference for "Wootton", because the name Wodeton pre-dated the patronage of the Bassett family in our town.

In 1914 farming was an important part of daily life. Farms were principally devoted to arable production, dairy farming, pig rearing, and market gardening. They ranged in size from a small patch for market gardening to several hundred acres. Just a few years earlier, in 1907, the Primitive Methodist minister Reverend Tonks wrote a treatise on the Brinkworth Circuit, "Victory in the Villages", in which he described the farming community in and around Wootton Bassett with admirable clarity:

> The farms are now almost entirely given up to dairy productions (milk and cheese), cattle growing, pig rearing, and the requirements of the market gardener, and general prosperity is manifest. Smallholdings are common, small landowners are also, fortunately increasing, and independence of all kinds shows a cheering growth. As to wages, it is here as elsewhere. Some farmers pay, as wages, as much as they can, and employ as many men as they can; others pay what they must, and employ only as many as they are compelled. The former rejoice in common with

their "men", the latter grumble and toil till they've hardly time to pray.
Farm labourers' wages vary from twelve shillings with house and garden,
to 16 shillings with similar additions.[1] Marvellously thrifty are those
who, on the former so-called wage, can live in honesty and cheerfulness,
and rear a family. Where health is vouchsafed it can be done and is done,
but the advent of the gaunt spectre of continued ill-health has marked the
doom of thousands, and they have in the past, died, crushed by inevitable
poverty.

The High Street was a thriving centre of trade and entertainment for both its own residents and those of the surrounding villages and hamlets. It was often bustling with businessmen in suits and hats, labouring men, farmers, soldiers in khaki, ladies with long hemlines and beautiful hats, girls in white cotton smock dresses, boys in caps, long socks, and short trousers, and babies in huge perambulators. By at least 1917 the High Street had been tarmac sprayed, but it was still a rougher road than we are used to today. The 60 lime trees lining the High Street were presented to the town by Sir Ralph and Lady Eastwood of Vastern Manor in 1897 to commemorate Queen Victoria's Diamond Jubilee. They graced the High Street during the Great War, and do so still today, with poppies planted around them to mark the centenary of the Great War.

A visitor to the High Street would have seen just a handful of vehicles, including horse-drawn carts, a smattering of traders' hand carts, a taxi, and an occasional motor lorry. There were very few cars in Wootton Bassett at the beginning of the war, but gradually numbers increased, to the extent that the town eventually supported two dealers, A and T Strange, and Reeves and Freegard. The steady increase in vehicular

---

[1] £1 in 1914 is equivalent to about £94.27 in 2019. Via 'Measuring Worth', using the Retail Price Index, https://www.measuringworth.com/calculators/ukcompare/relativevalue.php.

traffic led to the introduction of Wootton Bassett's first car parking charges in 1915. At a Parish Meeting on March 25th, Francis Teagle complained that motor cars were being allowed to stand in the Market Place on market days, and he suggested that they should pay a toll for the privilege, particularly as they were there partly to avoid the expense of using a hotel parking area. If a tradesman stood in the Market Place with a basket of fish, explained Mr Teagle, he would have to pay a toll of 6d or 1s, while a motor car could remain there for two or three hours without the owner having to pay anything. The clerk pointed out that the motors were not for sale, so the comparison was invalid. Mr Maslin, however, agreed with Francis Teagle. He felt that the motorists would rather pay a toll than be hustled by the police, which had been known to happen. The resolution was carried unanimously.

The town was lit by gas supplied by the Gas Company in Station Road. A rise in the price of coal necessitated a new contract for public lighting in July 1915. The price agreed with the Gas Company was £2 2s per lamp, with savings to be made by extinguishing lamps at 10pm instead of 11pm with no variation for phases of the moon.

The façades and layout of the High Street have altered very little, but beyond the town centre much has changed. Two major local employers of the day, the Dairy Supply Company and the Beaufort Brewery, have now gone, although a timber yard still exists at Vastern, where Twine Brothers operated during the war. The fields and hedgerows which used to abut the High Street in places have now been pushed far away from the town centre, and much agricultural land has been taken over by housing estates. On the fringes of the town during the war years, there were three marine store dealers, scrap merchants who bought and sold used waste materials including cordage, bunting, wool, rags, timber and metal. They were Charles Page in New Road, Ernest Camden on the High Street and Alfred Thompson at 46 Wood

Street. Today the commercial scene on the edge of the town is dominated by offices, light industry, modern engineering companies, and distribution centres.

Wootton Bassett was linked to Swindon by trade and employment, just as it is today. Swindon had grown hugely over the previous century, and by 1911 it boasted a population of 50,751. To put this in context, the current population of Swindon is over 200,000. The road between Wootton Bassett and Swindon was notoriously rough. Anthony Snow from Spittleborough Farm on the Swindon Road wrote to the Herald on December 30th 1919 and described the problem in detail:

The highway from Swindon to Wootton Bassett is like an old by-lane on a farm, where the manure carts are constantly travelling. It is in such an awful state that whether you are a pedestrian, cyclist or motorist, or the driver of a horse-drawn vehicle, you dread to have to go along that road. Only quite recently there have been cars there with broken axles, broken wheels and broken springs, motorcycles held up, and ordinary bicycles suffering fearfully from punctures, all caused by the terrible state of the roads. If something is not done quickly, the road will be impassable, for the holes make it like a switch-back to motorists and cyclists. Of course, this is such an outlandish road that I presume none of the members of the County Council ever pass along it!

In a later letter, he added that people frequently called at his house asking to borrow ropes to tow their broken-down vehicles into Swindon, or to borrow tools to repair their bicycles. In a reply, an anonymous "observer" wrote:

Prior to the County Council taking over the charge of the main roads I frequently rode on horseback with friends along the road Mr Snow complains of, and we had to go in file along the centre in places owing to the ruts. I noted carts broken down at various times. I measured the turf, which was allowed to grow over the metal for a width in many places of between one to three feet. When the county authorities took over control, I suggested that to save much hard labour, they should have it ploughed off with a team of horses, and this was done.

In mitigation, he said that the existing roads were never designed for the type of traffic now using them, in particular, the heavy weights pulled by hauliers, and he asserted that due to the war, the efforts of the council were frustrated by a lack of quality materials and adequate labour.

The locals would gladly travel to Swindon by rail instead of by road. Those who have been frustrated by cuts in local bus services over recent years will sympathise with the consternation felt in the town when in November 1917 the GWR discontinued one of the late trains which called at Wootton Bassett Station, just after 8 o'clock in the evening. The parish clerk was instructed to call the attention of the Great Western Railway authorities to the inconvenience caused by this.

Many Wootton Bassett folk travelled into Swindon to work for the Great Western Railway. Reverend Tonks wrote:

Some five or six hundred men and boys from the Circuit area find employment in the Great Western Railway Works there, and are accommodated by workmen's trains to Wootton Bassett and Purton, morning and evening.

In Wootton Bassett, a large number of the GWR employees were platelayers, whose job was to inspect and maintain the track. Most staff were paid weekly and had no job security. Looking through the 1911 census, one can easily imagine the pride of those who insisted on adding the word 'permanent' to their job description.

Among the ladies of the town, we find working women of every social class, including servants, dressmakers, milliners, laundresses, shop keepers, teachers, nurses, midwives and landladies. and one 'lady of the night'. Young boys in the town worked from the age of 13. They were often employed on farms, or as errand boys or delivery boys, but occasionally they landed a plum job as an apprentice in a local business. Girls too found work, mainly as servants and shop assistants.

At the beginning of the Great War, only a handful of telephones were installed in the town. The system was of the old type where a handle had to be turned. Using the Reading Phone Book for 1915 from the BT Archives and other contemporary documents I have compiled the following 'phone book':

Wootton Bassett 1 - Public Telephone Call Office

Wootton Bassett 2 - Doctor Watson

Wootton Bassett 3 - Radbone's Grocers

Wootton Bassett 4 - Beaufort Brewery

Wootton Bassett 6 - H Bevir's Solicitors

Wootton Bassett 7 - Smith and Hope

Wootton Bassett 8 - E H Edmonds

Wootton Bassett 9 - Railway Station

Wootton Bassett 10 - Dairy Supply Company

Wootton Bassett 13 - Police Station and Fire Station

Wootton Bassett 14 - Gerard Buxton, Tockenham Manor

Wootton Bassett 15 - William Drury, Butchers

Wootton Bassett 16 - Strange's Garage

Wootton Bassett 23 - Reeves and Freegard Motor Engineers

It was not until April 1925 that the telephone exchange in Wootton Bassett was upgraded to a 'modern' 240 line exchange powered by a gas engine and a dynamo, which provided automatic calling on lifting the receiver. As late as 1931 a new telephone customer was still sufficiently newsworthy that the Swindon Advertiser proudly published the names of businesses and private individuals having telephones installed.

There were no motor fire engines in the town during the great war. The fire pump was kept in a shed beside the police station and was dragged out by horsepower when required. It should be noted that the C18th pump displayed under the Town Hall is a much older one than that used in the Great War, and indeed, not local in origin. Its only credentials for being on display are that it had been there for so many years that it deserved to stay. In July 1918 concern was expressed about the long delay incurred when the Fire Brigade were called. This, it transpired, was due to the difficulty of providing horses to pull the pump . The Council would not entertain the idea of keeping horses in readiness, due to the expense, particularly as they might only be used once or twice a year. The Parish Council suggested that if farmers could send suitably harnessed horses along when they called on the Fire Brigade, much time would be saved, and the Council would be spared the cost of hiring horses.

The church was a major force in the daily life of Wootton Bassett, and much more prominent in public life than perhaps we are used to now. Three of the churches active during the Great War are still well known to us today: the Primitive Methodist Church on School Hill, the Parish Church in the High Street and the Congregational Church Meeting Place, now known as the United Reform Church, in Wood Street. There was a Wesleyan Chapel at the junction of Coxstalls and the High

Street. This was demolished in 1964 to make way for the widened road. There was also a small Baptist Church, the Hope Chapel, opposite the Infants School on School Hill. This was closed in 1939 and the space it left forms the side garden of a private house. Bible study classes for young men were held in the hall behind Fairview, and by 1920 the vicar's daughter, Miss Emilie Mathias, was running bible classes for the Parish Church.

Many clubs and groups were active in the town including the Oddfellows, the Ancient Order of Foresters who met at the Court House, the Women's Union, the Mothers' Meeting, the Red Cross, the Debating Society, and for young lads, the Boy Scouts. There was also a Wootton Bassett Branch for the National Union of Railwaymen.

Music played its part in town activities. I have not found evidence of any choir outside the church choirs, or an orchestra, but there was a popular town band, led by Levi Easley, who also played the violin. Levi was the man to turn to when you needed to put together an ad hoc orchestra. Three further groups seem to have formed just after the war: Percy Charles Mew formed a Choral Society, Sam Lawrence formed a Jazz Band which is mentioned in 1919, and a new 'Progressive Band' is mentioned in 1925.

Fig 1 - The Town Band with Bandmaster Levi Easley centre front, with thanks to RWB Town Hall Museum, Tony Sharp Collection.

I have found references to at least three music teachers in the town: Grace Bartlett, Gertrude Wallis, and Florence Mary Hart. Other active musicians included Miss Marchant (violin), Mr Bond and Mr W Parsons (cornets), Mr N Riddick (pianoforte),Miss Hilda Chequer (organ), Miss D Drury (piano), Mr L Tuck (piano), and William Timbrell Baxter (organ and double bass). Vocal soloists are often mentioned in the pages of the Herald, performing at events, concerts and services. Regular singers included Miss Watkins, Herbert Marchant, William Newton, the manager of the Dairy Company, Miss Beaven, Miss Van Rickstal (a Belgian refugee), headmaster Percy Charles Mew, Mr and Mrs F Watts, George Riddick, Mr C Chequer, Minnie Kench, and Miss E Chequer.

The ladies of the town seem to have had very busy and active social lives. Many took their community responsibilities very seriously, and the same names crop up again and again in the social diaries of the day. They organised fêtes, joined committees and undertook both local and international charitable work. They frequently held events and street

[45]

collections to raise money for national charities such as Alexandra Rose Day, Dr Barnardo's Homes, and a variety of Church Missions.

Hunting was a popular pastime among the upper classes in the Wootton Bassett area. There were two main Hunts in the area, the Beaufort and the Vale of the White Horse (Cricklade) known as the VWH. The Beaufort Hunt often rode through the land around Wootton Bassett and met in the town or at the Brewery. On August 18th 1914 Lord Beaufort wrote to the Herald with an announcement:

> Sir:- Owing to the present critical state of affairs, I am unable to make my usual arrangements as regards hunting this season. But I and all who hunt within my bounds are naturally anxious that no injury should arise from foxes, and I have therefore commenced cub hunting so as to kill down foxes. Should any further difficulties arise, I shall take an opportunity of taking the sense of the country as to what had best be done. Yours truly, Beaufort.

The VWH also announced changes due to the war. On September 4th the Herald published the following:

> According to present arrangements, there will be hunting two days a week as long as possible. Many horses from the kennels have been purchased for the Army, and the worthy Master (Major W F Fuller) is on service with the Wilts Yeomanry. Ted Goddard and Billy Pidden, first and second whips, have both volunteered for the New Army so that Willis will have a rather difficult task. Cubbing commenced on Tuesday at Hannington, some good sport being witnessed; a brace was accounted for. Reports go to show that there is an abundance of cubs all over the district. It is understood that the Countess of Craven will provide a bye-day occasionally.

If the licensing statistics are to be relied upon, in 1913 Wiltshire had the honour of being England's most sober county. The majority of drinking seems to have been convivial and restrained. The Petty Courts were well used to taking a hard line on drunken behaviour, or the inability of any landlord to control his customers. The temperance movement was growing increasingly influential at the time of the war. In Wootton Bassett, there was a local branch of the Great Western Railway Temperance Union, an occasional lecture or meeting, and the Band of Hope, a Christian children's group which encouraged them in the ways of temperance.

The Rechabites were a Friendly Society with a strong temperance ethos. A juvenile branch of the Rechabites opened in Wootton Bassett in June 1914. From this branch, a new adult 'tent' evolved the following year. About 200 guests attended the opening on Wednesday, November 24th 1915. The proceedings began with a tea for the juveniles, followed by a public lantern lecture at the Council Schools, presented by Chief Ruler Mr H G Summerhayes, of the Kingshill Tent, Swindon.[2] Mr Summerhayes explained the principles of Rechabitism and its benefits as a strong teetotal friendly society with over a million members and a positive bank balance. The new tent was established with twelve members, and the following officers were elected: Chief Ruler V Wiltshire; Deputy Ruler H Dixon; Past Chief Ruler W Brinkworth; Secretary George Mitchell of 29 Church Street; Levite F Woodward; Guardian D Mitchell; Steward H Hunt.

One might easily imagine that as the war progressed the local police were steeling themselves to crack down on the excesses of drinking, by soldiers, civilians in a state of heightened excitement, or those turning to drink to drown their sorrows. In the event, the war had little impact on the modest amount of alcohol-related crime in Wootton

---

[2] A lantern lecture was a popular entertainment in the war years. It consisted of a presentation at which illuminated glass slides were shown, with a spoken text or narration, and sometimes a musical accompaniment.

Bassett. Superintendent Millard presented his annual report at the Wootton Bassett Petty Sessions on 13th February 1915. There were 29 ale-houses, of which 16 were on-beerhouses, 5 were off-alehouses, and 6 were grocers' licenses. There had been only two prosecutions during the preceding year, for permitting drunkenness and for trading after hours. In every other case, the public houses had been well run, and all their licenses were renewed. There had been 16 proceedings for drunkenness in the area, which was one more than 1913 and four less than 1912. 11 of these resulted in convictions. The charges against one man, Reginald Creed,were dropped, as he had joined the Army.

Drinking in public houses was under control, but perhaps this masked a problem with drinking at home. The local annual report of the NSPCC was presented in November 1915. It revealed that of the 163 visits of supervision made in the district, 13 were in Cricklade and Wootton Bassett. Of the total cases, no fewer than 83 were due to drinking, involving 121 persons: 52 men and 69 women. Emily Harvey at 161 High Street was the most persistent offender.

Sometimes someone of 'no fixed abode' passed through the town, but they were swiftly moved on or directed to the workhouse at Purton. Superintendent Millard's 1914 report highlighted three tramps who were charged with drunkenness but were discharged on the condition that they left the town. In November 1915 a charge was brought against James Smith, age 43, that he had been found drunk and disorderly at Coped Hall on October 9th. The defendant did not appear, and the case was adjourned. He had been living in Wootton Bassett but was clearly itinerant in nature. Police Sergeant. Hillier explained to the magistrates that James had 'gone on tramp'. I have found no further record of him in the town.

Superintendent Millard's next annual licensing report was presented at Wootton Bassett Petty Sessions on 12th February 1916. There had been seven convictions for drunkenness in 1915, less than in 1914. Two licensed premises in the district had been fined for permitting drunkenness, but other than these two, the houses had been well conducted, and all licences were able to be renewed. The 1916 annual licensing report was presented by Superintendent Millard on 10th February 1917. There was one new club in the district at which intoxicating liquor was sold, which had received no complaints. No offences against the Licensing Act had been committed by any of the licensees, and all the houses had been conducted well. There had been only two charges of drunkenness at licensed premises, and both of these were made against the same female. On the first occasion, she was convicted, and on the second, a warrant was issued as she had left the district. The courts regarded this as a dramatic improvement on previous years. It seems that the combined effects of temperance and conscription had made the policeman's lot a very happy one.

There were two doctors based in the town, Dr Watson and Dr Fernie. A few wealthy families engaged private nurses to manage long term illness or old age. There were also two midwives in the town, who were available on call as required. The principal midwife, and possibly the best trained, as a member of the Central Midwives Board, was Mabel Emma Parke of 89 High Street and later 12 High Street. The other was Eliza Jane Beacham who lived at 29 Wood Street.

The poor and 'feeble-minded' of the town were cared for at the workhouse in Purton, managed by the Cricklade and Wootton Bassett Guardians. Their regular reports in the newspaper give some insight into the local medical provision, vaccination programmes, vagrancy, boarded out children, and clerical matters of local importance. In August 1915 the workhouse master Mr S W Maundrell reported that there were 40 inmates at the institution, compared with 57 the previous year, and the number of tramps given relief had dropped from 152 to 92.

The biggest political issue affecting Wootton Bassett, and the greatest challenge to the health of its people, was water supply and drainage. The drainage system was unsatisfactory and parts of the town, including Old Court, were still unconnected. The supply was also insufficient, with a good many connections yet to be made to the mains, and many houses still drawing their water from wells. The Dairy Supply Company needed a great deal of water to carry on its business, which caused more supply issues. The newspapers included interminable references to these issues. Heated discussions raged over many months, as local worthies debated the necessity for a better supply, and bemoaned the inevitable cost. The issue crept into every article and report from the Guardians, including the Medical Officer Doctor Watson's Annual Report for 1914, which was published in March 1915, in which he gave not only an excellent overview of health, mortality and housing in 1914, but also a summary of the water and drainage issues.

According to Doctor Watson, in the whole Cricklade and Wootton Bassett district, there were 247 births and 117 deaths in 1914. Causes of death included twenty-two people who died from disease of the heart, seventeen from pulmonary tuberculosis, eleven from malignant disease, five from pneumonia, two from scarlet fever, one from diphtheria, one from measles, one from tuberculosis meningitis, and one from another form of tuberculosis. There were also three deaths by violence and two suicides. Eleven deaths were of infants under one year of age. Of these, nine died from prematurity, marasmus and congenital malformation, one from infantile diarrhoea and one from icterus neonatorum. There was an outbreak of diphtheria in seven houses in Wootton Bassett resulting in fifteen cases. In five of the houses, the sanitary conditions were unsatisfactory, and in two cases the inhabitants were drinking water from polluted wells. The schools were closed in Wootton Bassett at the beginning of the year on account of the outbreak. There was an even bigger outbreak of measles in the Tockenham and Bradenstoke schools. 62 cases were notified, but thankfully, no deaths occurred. Infectious diseases were generally dealt with at the Isolation Hospital at Lydiard Millicent, but there were no facilities there to deal with more than one infectious disease at a time, so some cases of diphtheria and scarlet fever were sent on to the Isolation Hospital at Gorse Hill. Some new building had taken place in the Cricklade and Wootton Bassett district, including five new working-class dwellings, a children's home, a village hall, and a new milk factory. Twelve houses were found to be unfit for human habitation, and in all these cases, closing orders had been issued, but few had been implemented.

Lydiard Tregoze One Hundred Years Ago

Lydiard Tregoze parish curves in a banana shape around the north eastern boundaries of Wootton Bassett, dividing it from Lydiard Millicent, Swindon, and Wroughton. The Malmesbury Road and the Swindon Road separate it from Wootton Bassett, thus Coped Hall falls in Wootton Bassett and Marsh Farm falls into Lydiard Tregoze. It encompasses Hook, passes to the west and south of Lydiard Park, and continues to the present day motorway Junction 16 of the M4, where it meets Hay Lane and follows it down to its southernmost point at Basset Down.

The parish was a rural farming community throughout the Great War. The hamlet of Hook was the largest settlement in the parish. During the war, much of the business of the parish was transacted in the school. Hay Lane, now divided in two by the M4 motorway, was a rural artery running from north to south through farmland, dotted with farms and cottages, and neatly dissected firstly by the railway and secondly by the Wilts and Berks Canal. The canal was already disused by the beginning of the Great War and was formally abandoned by an Act of Parliament in September 1914. All the canal's land within the Swindon Corporation area became part of the Corporation's estate. Outside Swindon, ownership returned to the owners of the land adjacent to the canal.

The wharf, by the crossing of the canal and the lane, was a frequent meeting point for the huntsmen of the Vale of the White Horse Hunt (Cricklade). The Master of the Hunt from 1910 to 1931 was Colonel Fuller. He had brought his own hounds with him from Cattistock, and these, together with new hounds purchased by the Hunt committee, formed the nucleus of a pack to which many of the Hunt's current hounds still have bloodlines. Colonel Fuller shared the role of

Huntsman with Joe Willis, who held his post for 23 seasons. The present-day Hunt is particularly proud of its continuity of Masters and Huntsmen.

The parish had its own church, now within the grounds of Lydiard Park, and a burial ground provided by Lord Bolingbroke, on the road between Hook and Lydiard Park. There were also two nonconformist chapels in the parish, a small iron chapel built on the Purton road in 1886, and the Primitive Methodist chapel in Hay Lane. For many years the Primitive Methodists in the area met in a small wooden hut in a meadow opposite the wharf. The Primitive Methodist minister at the time, William Bridgeman, who died in 1915, would walk from Shaw to the wharf to conduct mission services. He often made house calls to the locals, delivering a tract, and offering advice and support to any who needed it. Eventually, Neville Story Maskelyne of Basset Down house donated some land, and in 1897 a galvanised iron mission room seating 75 was built beside the old hall by Thomas Colborne, the Swindon builder and timber merchant, at a cost of £80. By 1918 Hay Lane had an active and committed congregation from a wide area including Mannington and Toothill. There were an efficient Sunday School, a Band of Hope, and a Christian Endeavour Society connected to the chapel. Sadly neither of the chapels exist today.

The parish council was formed in 1894, and many of its meetings seem to have been concerned with the ownership and maintenance of the burial ground. A rather rude letter to the editor published in the North Wilts Herald of July 26th 1918 shows how low the parish had sunk and how desperately it needed to attend to its failings.

Sir, - One day last week I chanced to go through the little village of Hook whilst out for a stroll, and I could not help wondering if there were any sanitary inspectors in the district, for the offensive smells throughout the village were abominable. If all the people went down with typhoid, I

[53]

should not be surprised. When I go there again, I shall arm myself with a gas mask. I trudged down past the village school towards Lydiard Park, and on the way, I thought I would just have a peep at the little burial-ground, where many old friends of mine are resting. When I last saw it about 18 months ago, it was a well-kept little spot, but now it is in a very unkempt condition. It is, in fact, a disgrace to any parish or community. Yours truly, A PASSER-BY.

A terse reply followed quickly from Owen Hale of Creeches Farm:

Early in 1915, I was invited to undertake the care of the cemetery, and I agreed to do so. When it was first made, the late Viscount Bolingbroke gave a half-acre of land to the parish, and the cost of the buildings and enclosing - in fact of all the work appertaining to it - was paid out of the local rates. But I believe there was a clause in the deeds that gave the Rector a right to fees and the parish sexton to dig the graves. At the beginning of 1916, the place had fallen into a very bad condition, the graves being overgrown with bushes and brambles. I undertook to have the ground put into decent condition, and canvassed the parish for subscriptions, and everyone, with a few exceptions, contributed, the Nonconformists being particularly liberal. I got labour, and worked hard myself, and put the place into decent condition. When that was done the Rector insisted that it was a churchyard and not a cemetery, and referred to it as such in the Church Magazine. He and I have differed on that point, and always shall, as I fail to see how it can be a churchyard when it was provided out of the local rates and public subscriptions.

Emigration

One of the aspects of life in pre-war Wootton Bassett which would perhaps surprise today's reader was the strength of the pull to emigrate, particularly to Canada or, to a lesser extent, Australia. The local papers often ran advertisements about emigration, aimed especially at women in domestic service and men who wanted to be farmhands. The adverts were placed by government agents, shipping companies and railway companies. They seemed to reach a peak in 1913, for example:

> ONTARIO - *Farmers and Farm Hands Wanted. To any qualified man willing to work on the land, employment is guaranteed at good wages. Domestic servants are greatly in demand, wages £2 to £4 per month. Twenty million acres of Crown Land waiting for settlement.*

Another read:

> *Australia wants Farmers and Farm-Workers. Millions of acres of fertile lands. Wide choice of rural industries. Fertile lands on easy terms. Low cost of production. A healthy and sunny climate. Good wages to farmworkers with early prospect of acquiring freehold farms.*

A particularly long-running advertisement showed an illustration of a wheel with the word Canada in the centre. Each spoke bore a slogan promoting the benefits of the country:

> *Union Jack, Healthy Climate, Free Schools, Opportunity, Cheap Land, Light Taxes, Prosperity, Sunshine, Bread for All, Liberty, Good Wages, Profitable Farming, Free Land, Guaranteed Work, Rich Investments, Free Churches.*

In a time when the newspaper had very few illustrations or photographs, these bold adverts must have made quite an impact, particularly on disillusioned young men growing up in the rural communities around Wootton Bassett. In February 1913 a lecture was given by Mr E E Carleton at the Mechanics Institute in Swindon, on "Canada, the land of great possibilities and opportunities," which interested parties could attend to learn more. Occasionally the local papers featured letters from successful emigrants offering the benefit of their experience. A large party of emigrants who left the Great

Western Railway Works in June 1913, and one of its members published a letter recommending the working ethos in Canada:

> *The first thing that strikes the Englishman is the complete absence of caste in the workshop. There is an atmosphere of familiarity unknown in England. Manager, foreman and workman meet on almost equal terms; the whole staff pull together more as a team. The inefficient workman does far better in England than he does here (where) a man is judged solely by work done.*

Adverts were still appearing regularly in 1914, and it is little wonder that several of Wootton Bassett's young men left for Canada or Australia, looking for a better life. You will find some of their stories, which sometimes included service in the allied forces, in the companion volumes.

The Armed Forces

In 1914, as now, the Army was divided into regiments. Each regiment was divided into battalions, numbered 1st, 2nd etc.. As the battalions grew these were sometimes subdivided into further units, the 1st/1st and the 2nd/1st etc., where the subdivision is the first number and the main regiment is the second number.

Duke of Edinburgh's Wiltshire Regiment

The dominant local regiment was, of course, the Duke of Edinburgh's Wiltshire Regiment, often known as the Wiltshires, or simply the Wilts. The regiment was nicknamed the Moonrakers, affectionately by its members, and derogatorily by outsiders. According to local legend, customs officials had come across some Wiltshire bootleggers raking a pond to retrieve some kegs of contraband alcohol. The canny locals feigned stupidity, pointed at the reflection of the moon in the water and claimed that they were trying to retrieve a cheese. One of the old badges of the Wiltshire Regiment comprised two rakes crossed, with the barrel and moon of the Moonraker legend in the centre.

Early in 1914, the Wiltshires were 200 men below strength, and measures were being taken to encourage more recruits. On Monday 2nd March some 300 soldiers from Tidworth and a large number of Territorials from all the Swindon units paraded through Swindon. Their destination was the showing of a new film about the British army, presented by the Swindon branch of the Great Western Railway Temperance Union at the Great Western Railway Medical Fund Baths. The march was quite a spectacle, and the pavements were lined seven or eight deep with onlookers. The film started with a typical scene at a London recruiting station and continued with many cameos of army life. The audience, mainly soldiers, were especially impressed when a cavalry charge was shown.

[57]

A company burst right down the screen and appeared to leap away from the sheet right into the audience, the camera taking the film actually being knocked over.

The newspaper reported,

The picture was an excellent one, and should do a great deal to enliven the interest of the doings of the Army, and should certainly succeed in its main object - to attract and obtain recruits.

During the interval, Lieutenant Colonel Hasted explained that they wanted to recruit 200 men to keep up the numbers of the Wiltshires, because if they did not do so, the Regiment would be topped up by men from other counties and the Regiment would lose its county character. He wanted to see the county's Regiment composed entirely of Wiltshiremen. He provoked some laughter by admitting that he had heard whispers that Tidworth was not a good place to go as there were not enough girls there. But it was not a bad place - it was, after all, in Wiltshire.

In June 1914 the 1st Battalion of the Wiltshires went on a marching tour of the county to promote the service. The tour started from their base in Tidworth and proceeded to Devizes, Swindon, Chippenham, Trowbridge, Warminster, Salisbury, and home to Tidworth again. The stage was admirably set for the major recruiting campaign which would take place on the outbreak of war.

Under the arrangements created before the war during the Haldane Reforms, the regiment comprised two permanent battalions, the 1st and 2nd Wiltshires, and two reserve formations, one of which was a Special Reserve and the other a Territorial Force. Here is a brief summary of the locations of the Wiltshire's battalions at the beginning of the war.

1st Battalion Wiltshire Regiment

The 1st Battalion had returned to England in 1913 after five years in South Africa and were now based at Tidworth. Mobilization orders (instructions to assemble troops and supplies and make ready for war) were received on August 4th 1914. Over the 5th and 6th of August the men were inoculated against typhoid, and by the 8th of August mobilization was complete and the soldiers were awaiting commands. They did not have long to wait. On 13 August 1914, the battalion was transported by train to Southampton and was sent to join the British Expeditionary Force in France. Among them were a large number of soldiers from the Wootton Bassett area.

2nd Battalion Wiltshire Regiment

The 2nd Battalion had moved to Gibraltar in 1913. On 5 August 1914, at 2.25 in the morning, the battalion was notified that Britain was at war with Germany and were given orders to start mobilization. Within two hours they were called to action, with a corporal, ten men and some signallers being sent to take charge of two captured German merchant ships. On 16th August 1914, the battalion was notified to prepare to embark for England, bringing their peace and mobilization equipment with them. On arrival in England, it was remobilized, and in October 1914 it was sent to Belgium in defence of Antwerp.

3rd Battalion Wiltshire Regiment - The Special Reserve

The 3rd Battalion was the Wiltshire's Special Reserve. They were based in Devizes. Their service was similar to that of the Territorials, but unlike the Territorials, they were retained under the same conditions as the men of the Army Reserve, being enlisted for 6 years and having to accept the possibility of being called up in the event of a general mobilization. Significantly, they could also be sent overseas. The

Battalion comprised men who had already completed a term of service with the regular army and who could be called upon, if required, in an emergency. They were paid a retainer and had to attend a set number of training days per year. The Battalion mobilized in early August 1914. Many of the men went to fill up the needs of the 1st and 2nd Battalions. All those men surplus to these immediate requirements were posted to Weymouth, where they trained drafts for overseas service and carried out home defence and depot duties.

4th (Territorial) Battalion Wiltshire Regiment

The 4th (Territorial) Battalion was the Wiltshire Regiment's Territorial Force. They were fondly known as "Saturday Night Soldiers" as their members were all part-timers. The 4th Wiltshires were based at Trowbridge and trained units of men throughout the area. Wootton Bassett's closest unit was the Swindon unit, H Company, which was based in the drill hall in Prospect Place, Swindon. On the 4th August 1914, the 4th (Territorial) Battalion was mobilized and went immediately to Salisbury Plain. They were so oversubscribed that by October they had been subdivided into two Battalions, the 1st/4th and the 2nd/4th. The 1st/4th sailed from Southampton on the 9th of October and arrived in Bombay, India, on November 9th 1914. They later saw active service in the Egyptian Expeditionary Force. The 2nd/4th followed them to India and remained there throughout the war on garrison duties. A third Battalion, the 3rd/4th, formed a year later, in October 1915. They remained at home throughout the war, including service in the Dublin garrison.

5th (Service) Battalion Wiltshire Regiment

The Service Battalions were part of the so-called "New Army", which was raised and trained in wartime to support the four pre-existing permanent Battalions. The 5th was raised in Tidworth in August 1914.

After training, they were posted to the Dardanelles. They arrived in Gallipoli on July 17th 1915, and they were in the trenches fighting the Turks within two days of landing.

6th (Service) Battalion Wiltshire Regiment

When the 5th Battalion grew too large, the excess men were allocated to another new Battalion, the 6th, which was raised at Devizes. They, too, were trained for service overseas. They arrived in France in July 1915, and they were immediately plunged into trench warfare at Laventie and Festubert.

7th (Service) Battalion Wiltshire Regiment

The 7th Battalion was raised in Marlborough by Lieutenant Colonel Walter Leslie Rocke, a retired officer of the 1st Wiltshires. They trained at Codford, spent the winter in billets in Marlborough, and moved to Sutton Veny for final training in April. They sailed for France in September 1915 and spent two months in the trenches before moving on to Salonika.

8th (Service) Battalion Wiltshire Regiment

The 8th was unique among the Wiltshire Battalions as it was not a local battalion and no Wootton Bassett men served in it. It was formed from volunteers at Weymouth in November 1914 and was converted into a reserve battalion and absorbed into the 8th Reserve Brigade at Wareham. The battalion never deployed overseas.

3rd Wessex Brigade, Royal Field Artillery

There were two units of the 3rd Wessex Brigade of the Royal Field Artillery based at the drill hall in Prospect Place, Swindon. These were the Wiltshire Battery and the 3rd Wessex Ammunition Column. The Wiltshire Battery was a 1st Line Territorial Force. They were posted to India in late 1914.

The Wiltshire (Fortress) Royal Engineers

The Wiltshire (Fortress) Royal Engineers was a Works company and many local men from the Great Western Railway Swindon Works served in this unit. They were based at the drill hall in Prospect Place, Swindon. They later became the 1st/3rd Wessex Signal Company, Royal Engineers.

The Royal Army Medical Corps Field Ambulance

The Royal Army Medical Corps Field Ambulance was a specialist non-combatant medical corps, formed as a Home Service Brigade. They were based at the drill hall in Prospect Place, Swindon, and in Marlborough. The Brigade was attached to the 1st South Western Mounted Brigade of the Royal Wiltshire Yeomanry, which was based in Salisbury. It never saw active service. By 1915 it had been split up, all its regiments having been posted away.

The Army Veterinary Corps

The Army Veterinary Corps was a new Corps which was raised to look after sick and wounded horses. Captain J C Coleman was given the honour of raising one of the first contingents of the Corps in Swindon. Captain Coleman wanted 30 men, but in the event, he had at least 150 to select from. He chose on the basis of intelligence and the ability to learn the rudimentary principles of veterinary work. The men who joined the corps were all respectable young men, such as Clerks in the Great Western Railway Works and sons of tradesmen. The new corps presented a smart appearance when they paraded on the lawn at Captain Coleman's house. He told them that for the time being, he wanted them to forget their social positions and to remember that they were now soldiers, and as soldiers, he wanted them all to be brothers. They were to proceed almost immediately to Salisbury Plain for a course of instruction in veterinary work. Lectures would be given each day, and there would be drill, and if they could procure rifles, he would endeavour to get some shooting at the butts for them. They would all start off as Privates. Their progress through the ranks would depend upon the results of their examinations at the end of initial training, and their general aptitude and commitment thereafter. As they got their commissions so their pay would rise. After completing their probationary period, as Territorials, they would have the option of serving either at home or abroad. When they had sufficient training, they would be given a veterinary hospital of their own, where the wounded and sick horses would be sent for treatment.

The National Reserve

The National Reserve was a register of trained officers and men who had no further obligation for military service. Its purpose was to enable an increase in military resources in the event of imminent national danger. They were based in Devizes, and the closest Battalion to Wootton Bassett was the No.1 Swindon Battalion. Concerns had been expressed about the low strength of the National Reserve back in March 1914. Wiltshire had 108 Officers and 4007 men, but only 248 of these were Class 1, those who were willing to serve at home or abroad on mobilization. This represented only a fifth of the target number. The causes and remedies for this situation were still under investigation when war broke out.

Colonel Colston called the members of the National Reserve together in Devizes at very short notice. Over 300 responded, and there must have been several Wootton Bassett men among them. In the Market Place, an enormous crowd assembled. Colonel Colston addressed them all on the grave crisis, eulogising on the action taken by the Government and the magnificent speeches of Sir Edward Grey and Mr Redmond. He said that it was the duty of all men to forget party political divisions and to stand united for the Empire. He was cheered vociferously, and when he announced that although he himself was over age, he would gladly go if the authorities permitted it, the cheers rose again. A large number of younger men immediately volunteered for active service, and an even larger number volunteered for home defence. Fifty men were called for, to proceed to Salisbury on special duty. Enough men volunteered immediately to fill this requirement. The meeting ended with cheers for the King and for France.

The Royal Wiltshire Yeomanry

During the Boer War of 1899-1901, the Imperial Yeomanry was raised to allow Yeomen to serve overseas. The Royal Wiltshire Yeomanry provided three companies to this force (the 1st, 2nd and 63rd). On 17 April 1901, the name of the regiment was changed to the Royal Wiltshire Imperial Yeomanry (Prince of Wales's Own Royal Regiment). On the 1st of April 1908, the regiment was renamed again, becoming the Royal Wiltshire Yeomanry (Prince of Wales's Own Royal Regiment). It was transferred to the Territorial Force and from then on its soldiers were trained and equipped as Hussars, the mounted section of the Territorial Forces. Before the war, The Royal Wiltshire Yeomanry were based in Chippenham at The Butts and were divided into four Squadrons. C Squadron, which was based at Chippenham, had six remote detachments in Corsham, Malmesbury, Calne, Purton, Ashton Keynes and Wootton Bassett. Before the war, the Wootton Bassett detachment was based at a drill station in the town, but during the war, there was no activity in Wootton Bassett itself. In August and September 1914 the units were split into 1st Line for overseas service and 2nd Line for home service. Later, a 3rd Line was formed to act as a reserve,

The 1st/1st Royal Wiltshire Yeomanry was the 1st Line regiment. It was mobilized on 4th August 1914 as part of the 1st South Western Mounted Brigade, based in Salisbury. Initially, they were assigned to the Portsmouth defences, and then in October 1914, the brigade moved to the Forest Row area of Sussex where they were allocated to formations as required. Wootton Bassett's C Squadron, being part of the Chippenham HQ Squadron, was probably sent to join the 38th (Welsh) Division as they grouped at Winchester, and sailed to Le Havre on 4th February 1915. Their duties included policing, traffic control and despatch riding. The regiment played its part as cavalry only once, in March 1917, during the German retreat to the Hindenburg Line. In September 1917, it was finally conceded that there was little place for horsed cavalry on the Western Front and the remaining men, 14 officers and 232 other ranks, were transferred to the 6th Battalion of the Wiltshires.

The 2nd/1st Royal Wiltshire Yeomanry was the 2nd Line regiment formed for home service, for those unable or unwilling to serve overseas. It was raised in September 1914 and formed part of the 2nd/1st South Western Mounted Brigade. They stayed in England for the duration of the war.

The 3rd/1st Royal Wiltshire Yeomanry was a squadron-sized 3rd Line regiment. It was formed in 1915 to act as a reserve for the 1st and 2nd Line regiments, by providing trained replacements.

Royal Flying Corps

There were four Royal Flying Corps training aerodromes in Wiltshire: two at Yatesbury, built in 1916, to house two reserve (training) squadrons at each station. At this time, Netheravon (which replaced Larkhill as a Royal Flying Corps school in June 1913) and Upavon were the only other Royal Flying Corps training aerodromes within Wiltshire. On April 1st 1918, the Royal Flying Corps and the Royal Naval Air Service were amalgamated to form a new service, the Royal Air Force (RAF) under the control of the new Air Ministry.

The Armed Forces

The War Years - 1914

In a dinner and smoking concert arranged by the Discharged Sailors and Soldiers Federation in Wootton Bassett in March 1921, Howard Horsell proposed a toast to "The Navy and the Army," and added that, "the story of the immortal deeds of our brave lads against such overwhelming odds would be handed down to posterity". As with much family history, this was not to be. Within two generations, we had all but lost sight of the story of our local heroes and their homes and families. It was with some trepidation and a great sense of humility that I began to write their forgotten story.

From the beginning of the war, life in Wootton Bassett began to change in many ways, from the subtlest and smallest to the most dramatic and tragic. The following pages tell of some of the events which took place in the town during the war years. It is here that you will read about the work the townsfolk undertook in support of the forces, local events during the war years, acts of remembrance, celebrations of peace, and finally war memorials. Details of the casualties and those who served can be found in the companion volumes.

War was declared on 4th August 1914. Sadly no record survives to show how the news arrived in Wootton Bassett. It is likely that a telegram was sent to the telegraph office, or perhaps a telephone call was made to one of the few lines in town. Perhaps then a notice was put up in a council office window. Most probably a bell-ringer hurried to the church, and the tenor bell was tolled, as it was on other sombre occasions later in the war. The news must have spread rapidly from house to house, and the reservists who had been expecting the call to arms must have responded quickly, saying their farewells and rushing to Wootton Bassett station to travel into Swindon, or making their way to the Barracks at Chippenham or Devizes, not knowing for certain whether they would be home again that night.

On the streets of Swindon, a heady atmosphere of anticipation must have been evident all day. At 7.40 in the evening, the GWR hooter sounded out ten blasts to summon the Territorials to their headquarters. That hooter is still blown from time to time on rare special occasions. It is a truly haunting sound, and it puts a real lump in your throat to imagine how it would have been greeted by the families who heard it that night. The men changed quickly into their uniforms, and within half an hour, they started to throng to the Drill Hall in Prospect Place. The first meeting was short and to the point. Soon after 10pm the men were dismissed, with instructions to return the next day for medical examination.

On Wednesday 5th the men presented themselves at the allotted times for their examinations. As each one arrived, they were greeted by a huge crowd of about a thousand civilians, who had gathered around the Drill Hall, cheering and singing patriotic songs. Another crowd had assembled at Swindon station, where reservists were setting off in large numbers throughout the day, to rejoin their various regiments and headquarters around the country. The gathering was excited but orderly, and every so often they broke into a rousing rendition of Rule Britannia. In every corner there were emotional farewells.

The main body of the Swindon Territorials departed at 6pm by the Midland and South Western Junction Railway. They had spent the day transporting their guns and ammunition from the Drill Hall to the station so that everything was ready. As they paraded, the cheers rose from the crowd again and again. Finally, the Mayor of Swindon, Mr C Hill, gave a stirring farewell speech. He concluded:

Our good wishes go with you, believing that you will, as worthy sons, uphold the best traditions of our forefathers. We feel sure you will always be at the place where duty or danger calls. What we say to you, we say to your comrades who have gone on in advance, to those who are to follow you, and also to those who have gone to active service straight from Camp without the opportunity of coming back to Swindon and saying good-bye to their friends. Be of good cheer, goodbye, good luck and God bless you all.

At this the cheers arose, louder than ever. The Swindon Advertiser describes it thus:

Many pathetic scenes were witnessed during the last moments between the young fellows and their relatives. All the men looked in the best of condition and were fine types of English manhood, and we feel sure, if they are needed, will not be found lacking in courage or ability and continue to hold the good name they have already earned and that of the Wiltshire soldier in general.

For a few days, mobilization orders brought wave after wave of young men into the town, and the residents watched them go in scenes which varied from utter grief and despair, through 'putting a brave face on it,' to eagerness and excitement.

On August 7th the Herald published all the details of the mobilization. In this era of sensationalism and bold headlines, it is hard to countenance that news of the war crept into their pages with relatively little drama. An inside page declared, "Nations at War, The Sword Drawn. Kaiser Strikes First Blow. British Plans." The papers during that first week published a letter from Mr E T Knapp, local secretary and staff officer of Swindon's No 1 Battalion of the National Reserve, listing the opportunities available to National Reservists wishing to volunteer. 200 men were required for the Army Veterinary Hospital in

Salisbury. Others were required for the local Territorial Units including the Royal Wilts Yeomanry, the 3rd Wessex Brigade Royal Field Artillery, the Wilts (Fortress) Royal Engineers, the 4th Battalion of the Wiltshire Regiment, T and S Columns, the Army Service Corps, Field Ambulance, Royal Army Medical Corps, and other units. He encouraged men to come into the Drill Hall in Church Place in Swindon, to send in their registered numbers, names and addresses, update their details, and await further information.

After the departure of the last of the Swindon Royal Wiltshire Yeomanry on Sunday afternoon, very few 'citizen soldiers' were left in Swindon, but the complexion of the town quickly changed as regular troops from other parts of the country swarmed in and out. The Advertiser described Swindon as having the appearance of a garrison town. By the end of August, gentlefolk were already expressing concerns about the behaviour of young people in Swindon. 'A A' wrote to the Editor of the Swindon Advertiser in no uncertain terms:

Walking down Regent Street last Monday night about 8.30, I was amazed at the number of young girls escorted by soldiers. Many of these girls are very pretty, with the bloom still on their cheeks. I heard one laugh; it was very innocent. I think I must have met forty couples at various stages. In two cases, the girl had her waist encircled by a soldier's arm, yet everybody smiled tolerantly. Where have these young girls sprung from? I am not speaking prudishly. But it is appalling to notice that scarcely one of these girls counts more than 17 summers, and many are apparently younger. It would appear that both sides are having a "joy time". These girls could not have known these men before last Sunday night. While we wish to be hospitable and kindly to the defenders of our fair land, we must not forget that these sweet girls are the future mothers of Britain's children, and it is a pity to spoil their young lives with the fleeting passions that come and go, as "ships that pass in the night."

The Technical School, Higher Elementary School, Westcott School, and Ferndale Road School were all requisitioned as mess rooms for the soldiers. Appeals were published inviting civilians to contribute to the war effort in whatever way they could. Many householders were asked to billet as many as five or six soldier guests, and they must have been glad to comply, both from patriotic duty and because they were paid for the service. Regrettably, I have not found records of any premises used as billets in Wootton Bassett, but there must have been many occasions when soldiers were accommodated in the town as they passed through.

Away from the excitement and energy of the town centre, groups must have gathered in the pubs, clubs and churches, discussing the developing situation with varying degrees of concern, sadness and shock. Many of the older generation had been engaged in the Boer War in South Africa, and their attitude to a further conflict was understandably cautious and guarded. However, the excitement must have been infectious, and before long even the most cynical must have been imbued with the sentiment of patriotic camaraderie and determination which pervaded all corners of the county. In rural communities, too, the loss of many fit young farm labourers to the ranks of the forces was an immediate concern. The advent of the war coincided with a pressing requirement to bring in the harvest. Aware of the delicacy of this issue in rural Wiltshire, the Members of Parliament for Wiltshire, Basil E Peto, Geoffrey Howard, Godfrey Locker-Lampson, George Terrell, Richard C Lambert, and Charles Bathurst published a letter in the local press:

The Country has immediate need of 100,000 men to join the ranks of the Army. They are to be enlisted for the Army, not for special branches, and allotted as the War Office thinks best. All particulars can be obtained at the Post Offices and Military Depots. We venture to appeal to the people of Wiltshire to give an immediate and generous response to this appeal. It is inevitable that if the appeal is successful, great inconvenience must be caused, of a serious character to local work of all kinds, and we suggest that in every village a Committee should be formed to so organise things that the places of men who join the ranks shall be filled by volunteer labour or by the assistance of those who do not ordinarily take part in these operations. Gardeners, stablemen, etc. can with great advantage be all turned onto field work, as it is of vital importance that every effort should be made to secure the food supply in order to prevent the loss which would add to the possible prospective shortage.

Recruitment

The first recruitment meeting in Wootton Bassett was held on the Sunday afternoon of August 30th 1914, at the Police Court. The meeting was well attended and was led by three of the top brass in the region: Admiral William Wilson of Clyffe Pypard Manor House, Colonel Thomas Charles Pleydell Calley, and Major F P Goddard of The Lawn Manor House, Swindon. They were supported by Mr E Pritchard, Mr J Moore, Captain Chute of the Recruiting Staff and Dr S Maclean.

Fig 2 - Colonel T C P Calley campaign photo 1910, with thanks to Swindon Museum and Art Gallery.

Colonel Calley was a Unionist and had been MP for Cricklade in 1910. His estate, Burderop Park, near Chiseldon, had already become a military training camp. He delivered a stirring, if lengthy, appeal to the people of Wootton Bassett, which the North Wilts Herald reported in full:

> *At a time like this, it is everybody's business to come forward and help the country. At the present moment, party politics are dead and done away with; all is for the State. We must stand shoulder to shoulder.*

There might be, and are, many who do not know anything about the cause of the war, and some might say they do not want war. We are a peace-loving nation, we have a large Empire, and we do not want any more territory. We are a Christian people and war is a denial to Christianity. No-one should go to war unless there is a just reason. Some might say "Why are we fighting for Servia (sic)?" We are not fighting for Servia. That Servia is the cause of the war we admit, but the real cause of the war is the aggression of Germany. No nation has made such a pretence of maintaining the peace of the world or talking so much about friendship for England, and yet at the same time, Germany has been arming for the purpose of placing us and other nations under her heel - the heel of aggression and despotism. Lord Roberts, who has been like the voice of one crying in the wilderness, for many years has been telling us that we are not safe, and has advocated a scheme for training the young men of the country. Now we find ourselves in the midst of a great and terrible war and have to make an urgent appeal for men. We are at war for two things chiefly, firstly honesty and honour, and secondly our interest and our lives and existence as a nation. First, our honour is involved through the neutrality of Belgium, which as a state was guaranteed by the great Powers of Europe, and one of the chief signatories was Germany. Yet the moment Germany saw her chance she said: 'What is a treaty - a piece of paper that can be torn up!' But not so with Britain. We have given our pledged word and will back that up by all the force in our power. We will stand to our word.

This proclamation was met with cheers. Calley continued:

Secondly, supposing we had shown the white feather and said we would not oppose Germany. When Germany had over-swept Belgium and brought France to her knees, England would have been next, and the horrors of Belgium would have been ours. If such had been the case, no nation in the world would have helped us. So it was perfectly plain that

*no Briton could deny that honesty and honour and our interest and
existence had brought us into this conflict. We have for years disregarded
the words of men who knew their words were true. We do not need an
army to make war, but for the protection of our country and our Empire.
We have been told that to have a system of training such as Lord Roberts
advised would interfere with the financial interests and the general
progress of the country. The untrained man is not only of no use in time
of war, but is a danger. We require an Army so strong that it could be
landed to any foreign country and give a good account of itself. We have a
good Navy, but anyone who is an authority would say that a strong
Navy was not good enough and that we must have a strong Army as
well. We do not like to look on the black side of things, but it is quite
certain that the Army we have sent to France will be seriously depleted,
large as it is. Therefore we must have men trained and ready to take the
places of those who will go to reinforce that Army. If the Germans get
much nearer the coast of France, it might be possible for them to land a
force on our shores. We must remember that it was the British nation
that foiled Napoleon at every point and at last brought him to his knees.
Therefore let us as Britons put all our private interests on one side and go
and serve our country. If we fail now to answer our country's call, let us
forever hide our heads for shame. Those who have others dependent on
them can rest assured that the nation will look after them. I appeal for all
who are eligible to come forward and answer the call.*

After Calley's speech, Captain Chute took the stand. He explained that
the terms of service were for three years or for the duration of the war,
and that they would be released as soon as possible after the war was
over. Major Goddard strongly endorsed the remarks of Colonel Calley
and emphasised the fact that we had to fight until we had absolutely
beaten the Germans or until there was not a man of us left. At the end
of the meeting, several young men came forward and gave their names.

It wasn't long before voices in Wiltshire rose to condemn those who did not join up. A letter to the editor in the North Wilts Herald on August 28th 1914 put it strongly:

We do not want a blot on the British name by having a "blue-funk brigade" lagging behind in our towns and villages. At the present time, the apathy of seemingly eligible young men to be seen promenading the streets and elsewhere is appalling.

By September many lads from Wootton Bassett and the surrounding area had responded to Lord Kitchener's call and joined up. On the 4th the local correspondent for the Herald, Miss Guy, wrote:

Quite a large number of reserves from the district have gone to the front, and during the last week, several young men have joined Lord Kitchener's Army.

A week later The North Wilts Herald published a list of the 47 men who had been the first to enlist in the Wootton Bassett area. Many were Reservists who had served in the Wiltshire Regiment in India or South Africa; others were raw recruits. On August 14th 1914 six of these Wootton Bassett men had arrived on the Western Front. Only one of them would return safely.

Recruitment in Lydiard Tregoze

Some of the lads of Lydiard Tregoze had already enlisted when an enthusiastic meeting was held on the evening of September 7th 1914 at the School Room in Hook in support of Lord Kitchener's call to arms. Presiding over the meeting was Frederick Leighton, schoolmaster and chairman of the parish council. He addressed the meeting himself, as there was no guest speaker. He described the reasons why Britain was at war and expressed the need and urgency of the appeal for men. He urged that it was the duty of every man to come forward at this time of national emergency. Both of Frederick's sons would serve in due course. Concerned about the sprawling nature of the parish, the attendees decided to appoint a committee of six men whose role would be to impress duty upon the young men in their own local areas whenever they encountered them. The committee comprised Edward Hiscock, Hervey William White, Mr Cole, Mr Large, Mr W O Titcombe and Frederick Leighton. The same committee were also charged with collecting information about those who had already gone to the front, leaving dependants behind. Frederick Leighton advised that those whose husbands had been called up or had enlisted, and those who had lost the means of support for their household due to the departure of a man on whom they were dependent, would be invited to come forward and identify themselves to the members of the committee. Edward Hiscock and Frederick Leighton, who were the appointed representatives of the parish on the District Relief Committee, were particularly anxious that nobody should be overlooked, and that the absence of a breadwinner should not cause distress or privation to those left at home. Finally, Edward Hiscock was appointed as the representative of the parish on the Central Committee at Swindon. The meeting closed with the singing of the National Anthem.

The YMCA

The YMCA in Wootton Bassett was launched in December 1907 and was already well established in the town when war broke out. The bible class was regarded as the foundation of the association. It was held in the building behind Fairview, 56 High Street, Alfred Ricks Humphries' home, and on the lawn in the summer, and was well attended. It was a matter of pride to the association that several young men had taken up positions as Sunday School teachers and were taking an interest in 'higher things'. From 1912 two rooms in London House, 126 High

Street, were set aside to be used by the YMCA as a reading and activities area. It was also proposed that a YMCA gymnasium should be set up in the town. I believe that the gymnasium was established at the little hall in Sparrow Lane by 1913. In 1913, Mr Bevir, the Chairman, commended the association highly. He said that it was a good thing that older folk should be brought into close friendship with the boys as they grew up, especially those who would not otherwise be brought into contact with the younger generation. He stressed how important it was that a boy should choose the right friends, ones who could be relied on to help him in times of trouble and warn him to keep away from what was wrong. Some young people, he said, looked with little reverence on some of their old grey-haired friends, and thought they were old fogies, yet they ought to find amongst the older people friends who they could trust and depend upon in times of trouble. The members would find that the association would make their lives more useful, it would make them better members of society, and would help them to fill their places in life, and when they grew older, they themselves would be able to lend a helping hand to the younger ones. His speech was met with several bursts of applause.

In 1914, the YMCAs of the region swung into action to support the troops, setting up three large marquees at Chiseldon Camp, and a writing, reading, games, and refreshments room in the Conservative Club in Fleet Street, Swindon. Their hope was to offer men away from home everything possible to make their leisure time profitable and enjoyable and give them some comfort, making it easier for them to write home by providing free reading and writing materials, and helping them to keep straight amidst new and strong temptations. They appealed to the public for any gifts which would make their premises more attractive and comfortable for the troops, including magazines, books, songbooks, pictures, cushions, vases, gramophones and records, armchairs, billiard tables and of course, contributions in cash.[3]

The Boy Scouts

Fig 3 - Wootton Bassett Scouts postcard, copyright unknown

Of all the young people in Wootton Bassett, it was perhaps the Boy Scouts who played the most enduring part in the War. During the Boer War Baden-Powell had been struck by the idea that youngsters could be used as messengers, scouts and watchmen. He launched his first Boy Scout Camp in August 1907 on Brownsea Island. Wootton Bassett was one of many towns which formed their own troop as the movement gathered impetus. Howard Horsell and Alfred Ricks Humphries were foremost amongst those who founded the troop. A public meeting was called to establish the group in the assembly room of the Angel Hotel on Saturday, 19th March 1910. The first meeting

---

[3] There is more information about the YMCA in the Town companion volume under the entries for Fairview, 56 High Street, and London House, 124 High Street.

was convened at the same venue a few days later, on Wednesday, 23rd March. Forty-five boys were enrolled, with Mr J Brown as Scout Master and Mr Beacham (probably Reginald Beacham) and Mr Smith (probably Henry Smith) as Assistants. The first President would be Alfred Ricks Humphries, of Fairview, 56 High Street.

Scouting was not always a serious occupation. For many of the boys, the chief incentive for membership must have been the exciting range of activities on offer. However, it is almost certain that the lads were encouraged to feel that they were preparing to serve their country, as many of them would go on to do. On the Bank Holiday weekend before the war began, between the 1st and 3rd of August 1914, Howard Horsell's lake, now Jubilee Lake, was the venue for an exciting swimming competition. The races included categories for Wootton Bassett Scouts alone and for all-comers. There were swimming races for Scouts under 15, Scouts over 15, and men, with distances from 25 yards to 100 yards, and diving competitions. Novelty events included a duck hunt and 'walking the pole', each with the prize of a couple of fat ducks. There were contests for the smartest and best Scout Patrols, the best all-round Scout, the best signaller, and the best ambulance skills. The event closed with a display by the Swindon and Wootton Bassett Scouts. At the end of the evening, prizes were distributed by Mrs Mary Arnold-Forster of Basset Down.[4] A very encouraging address was given by her son, John Arnold-Forster. Finally, a hearty vote of thanks was proposed by Howard Horsell to Mrs Arnold-Forster, which was "carried with cheers by the company". The Herald reported:

Notwithstanding the very inclement weather, the Aquatic Sports which were held on Bank Holiday at The Lake, Wootton Bassett, by kind

---

[4] For more about Mrs Arnold-Forster see Bassett Down in the the Country companion volume.

[80]

permission of Mr H Horsell and Mr B Sergeant, were a great success.
There were not quite so many entries in some of the events as one would
have liked to have seen, but on the whole, a very enjoyable time was spent.

The very next day, the war began, and the Scouts took up activities of
a very different kind. The Herald published an update on "What the
Boy Scouts are Doing" on August 14th 1914. Although the article
refers to Swindon rather than Wootton Bassett, it gives a good flavour
of the mood which pervaded the movement and the type of tasks in
which Wootton Bassett's Scouts must also have been engaged:

In this time of national emergency comes the opportunity for the Boy
Scouts organisation to show that it can be of material service to the
country, and the Scouts of Swindon, who number upwards of 200, are
embracing it with both hands. Lieutenant General Sir Robert Baden-
Powell, who is at the head of the movement, has organised a scheme of
non-combatant service, and the lads are proving themselves exceedingly
useful. The Corporation has placed a committee room at the Town Hall
at their disposal, and Mr W Arnold-Forster (a son of the former
secretary for War) is acting as Scoutmaster and setting the youngsters a
splendid example by his wholehearted enthusiasm and zeal. Ever cheerful
and ever alert, the Scouts are demonstrating that they can render valuable
assistance to the State at home, and for this their training and
organisation have already to a great extent fitted them. The duties which
they are performing consist chiefly of distributing circulars for the
Corporation and taking soldiers to their billets. A corps of cyclist
messengers has been established, and the Scouts have offered their services
to the Post Office and the Great Western Railway Company at any time
they should be needed. These lads never seem to tire. They are running
about from early morning to late at night, rendering whatever assistance
they can, and people who have been wont to scoff at them are now freely
acknowledging the utility of the movement. During the last few days, the

committee room at the Town Hall has been open all night for telephone communication, and no fewer than 10,000 circulars have been distributed in the town.

Normal Scouting activities continued throughout the war, but with a more military flavour than we would recognise today. Members of the Wootton Bassett Troop met on the lawns of Fairview in the High Street on the evening of July 11th 1916, to be presented with proficiency badges by the Commissioner, Mr W R Bird, before an audience of parents and friends, and the Scouts gave excellent displays of dumbbells, signalling, ambulance and Indian clubs. One of the special guests at this event was a former Scout who had taken part in the naval Battle of Jutland. This was probably William Newman of 54 Church Street. Mr Bird delivered a very encouraging and helpful speech. A vote of thanks was given to Howard Horsell, thanking him for the use of the lake for swimming, the rifle range for practice, and the free use of ammunition. The proceedings ended with hearty cheers for the King and for Mr Bird.

The 2nd Troop of Boy Scouts from Swindon visited Wootton Bassett on January 23rd 1918 to participate in a huge gathering. The fall-in sounded at the Town Hall, and the Swindonians then marched up the High Street behind their own fife and bugle band, who played 'Marching through Georgia'. On arrival at the Board School which hosted the event (it is not clear where this was, but probably the Manor House) there was a musical display and a general salute. The house was packed with friends, families, and guests. The first half of the programme was supplied by the Wootton Bassett Scouts, led by Scout Leader Brust and Miss Lucy Humphries. They performed some dumbbell exercises, the songs 'Carry On' and 'Fall In' and a display of ambulance work. The Swindon Scouts provided most of the second half, which included songs and sketches, rifle drills, some particularly impressive sword-swinging, and gymnastics. The Swindon boys were provided with an excellent tea, and a very enjoyable evening was had by all.

The YMCA held a special remembrance meeting of the Bible Class in connection with the Boy Scouts at the YMCA Hall behind Fairview on Sunday, 15th September 1918. A good number of parents, boys, and friends attended. Special prayers were said, and hymns were sung in honour of the lads who had made the greatest sacrifice for the freedom of the world. The Chairman, Howard Horsell, made a cheering speech to the Scouts and exhorted them to courage, discipline, and the fear of God. Next, a visitor, Mr W T Wiltshire, gave a special address. He was a lay reader from Stanton Fitzwarren, an old officer of the Church Lads' Brigade, and a Scoutmaster in Derbyshire. His text was 'Blessed are the pure in heart'. He summarised the origin and course of the war and paid a warm tribute to the Scouts and other lads of the town who had given their lives and service for God, truth, and right. He was certain that great good would come of the war. He urged that the real measure of success would depend upon both the purity of purpose of England and her allies and the individual purity of each man and lad. Mr Alfred Humphries read out a list of Scouts who had gone on active service, mentioning especially the dead heroes. By that time fifty Wootton Bassett Scouts had gone to the front, of whom six had laid down their lives. The National Anthem was sung at the close.

On Tuesday 17th September 1918 the Scouts met on the lawn at the Manor House where they were presented with their awards for the preceding half year. Among these were Scout V Leighfield and 14-year-old Edward Parke, the son of Nurse Mabel Parke, who had earned their Ambulance Badges. Edward Parke had also earned his

Interpreter Badge, and Scouts Blackwell, Reeson, and Barnes had earned their Thrifty-Men Badges for war savings.

After the war, the Scouts continued to meet at Fairview and later at the hall in Sparrow Lane. It was not until 1959 that they obtained the present site in Muddy Lane, which was donated by a local farmer. The money needed to build a large prefabricated hut on the land were supplied by a King George VI trust fund supplemented by a great deal of enthusiastic fundraising.

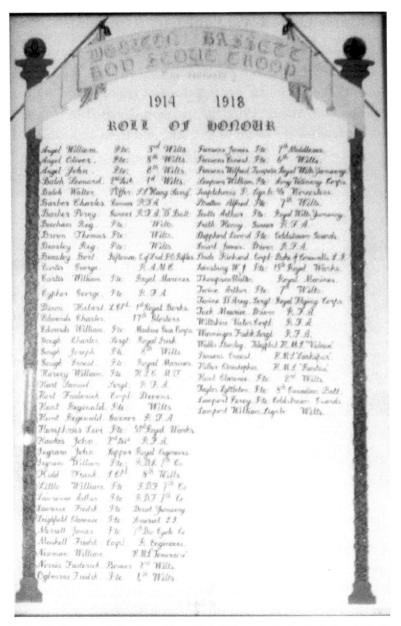

Fig 4 - Wootton Bassett Boy Scout Troop Roll of Honour, with thanks to Royal Wootton Bassett Boy Scouts

The King's Own Royal Lancaster Regiment

One of Wootton Bassett's earliest encounters with troops came with the arrival of the 1st/5th Battalion, King's Own Royal Lancaster Regiment. The Regiment was mobilized at Lancaster on 4th August 1914. On 14th August 1914, the battalion departed from Lancaster Castle Station for the south of England, and from 15th August 1914 to October 1914 they served in Didcot and the surrounding area, guarding lines of communication including the railway station and bridges in Wootton Bassett.

Fig 5 - The 1st/5th King's Own Royal Lancaster Regiment guarding the Railway at Wootton Bassett in 1914, with thanks to King's Own Royal Regiment Museum, Lancaster.

The soldiers were given a warm welcome in Wootton Bassett. Regimental correspondence reveals that they were customers of King and Sons the harness makers. Individual residents who did their bit for the visitors included Julie Morgan of Priory Cottage, 28 Wood Street, who opened her home to the young men for rest and recreation. On a Tuesday evening in October 1914, a Smoking Concert was held in the

Red Lion Assembly Rooms to entertain the Lancasters. Howard Horsell presided, supported by Reverend Martyn Roberts, curate at Sherborne Abbey, Reverend B Edwards, and James Frank Underhill. The musical programme included performances by both local residents and the soldiers. There was a good attendance, and everyone enjoyed a very pleasant evening, with refreshments provided. The battalion made many friends while they were billeted in the area and some soldiers kept in touch with the locals after they were posted on to Sevenoaks, Kent, in October 1914. They sailed for Le Havre on 15th February 1915. On June 4th 1915 the Herald reported on their progress at the front in France:

> *That they have proved themselves to be brave and undaunted in the fight is proved by the fact that Sir John French warmly praised the regiment who were in the fierce fighting round Ypres. The original battalion strength has been reduced to eight officers and about 200 men.[5] Among the officers who are unofficially reported killed is Captain M Bingham, a popular Lancaster doctor. He went through the severe fighting in the earlier part of the month around Ypres and had three days furlough to visit his wife and little children last week. He was killed while on reconnoitring work the day after his return to the front.*

The Arrest of Germans

On August 27th the Home Office wrote to the War Office recommending the immediate arrest of any German and Austrian reservists of military age living in England. The suggestion was accepted, and the Home Office instructed the police to arrest any reservists who might pose a danger. By September 23rd there were 13,600 Germans interned in camps around the country, of which

---

[5] At full strength a Great War battalion consisted of 1007 men.

10,500 were civilians. Most of the remainder were captured on the battlefield. One of these civilians was Wilhelm Faltermeier, who was arrested in Uffcott on September 8th 1914. Wilhelm was a restaurant proprietor at 114 Southampton Road, Eastleigh, Hampshire, who had formerly served in the German Army. He was born in Regensberg, Bavaria, in 1877, came to England and married Annie Hacker in 1905. They had two sons, Eugen and Harold, and a baby daughter, Gracie, who died in infancy. Harold was born in Uffcott in 1909, probably at White's Farm, and he was raised by his grandparents there. Wilhelm was visiting his son and in-laws, perhaps deliberately hiding there, when he was arrested. He was taken to the German Prisoner of War camp at Newbury under escort by a party of Territorials. Wilhelm later returned to his home and restaurant in Eastleigh. In December 1919 he was naturalised, and in July 1920 he changed his name to William Falter by deed poll. The only German resident who I have found in Wootton Bassett and the hamlets immediately around it was Susanna Jenny Paynter, whose mother was German and who was born in Germany.[6]

The Belgian Refugees

A Belgian Refugee Fund was quickly active in the Swindon area thanks to the diligent leadership of Mrs Arnold-Forster of Basset Down, who was the honorary secretary of the Swindon District Committee. Wootton Bassett had its own local committee, the members of which included Howard Horsell, George Marshall Watts, Sydney Cotton, James Frank Underhill, and Mr E Wallis. The Treasurer was Frank Bartlett of 140 High Street. From the outset, there was an excellent response to fundraising appeals in Wootton Bassett. The town's two Harvest Festival services on October 8th and 11th 1914 were

---

[6] For Susannah's story see Tockenham Wick in the country companion volume.

dedicated to the fund. The Church was filled with flowers, fruit, vegetables, ducks, rabbits, eggs, cakes, jam, tea, coffee, bread, and clothing of all descriptions, donated by parishioners and beautifully arranged by the ladies of the congregation. It must have been a magnificent sight, and the smell must have been glorious! Compare this to the drab piles of cans and boxes with which we celebrate a harvest festival today. The usually joyous harvest celebrations were tempered, however, with sorrow for the nation's losses on the battlefields. The Thursday service was conducted by the Reverend Martyn Roberts, visiting from Sherborne Abbey, who read with feeling from Psalm 127 'They that sow in tears shall reap in joy'. Reverend Mathias also chose appropriate sermons for the three Sunday services. All of these had strong attendance, and the collections were excellent. On the following Monday morning a cheque for £20 7s 6d was conveyed, free of charge, by James Taylor to Miss Blake, the secretary of the Fund at Swindon.

In late October 1914, Wootton Bassett's plans to host its own family of Belgian refugees were nearing fruition, and it was hoped that everything required would be in place in time for the family's arrival. The Dairy Supply Company had not only provided a property for the refugees rent-free but had also offered to give all the milk required. The upkeep of the house would be met by weekly subscriptions, and a number of ladies had made themselves responsible for collecting these. The committee also welcomed donations from anyone in the district, which should be sent to Frank Bartlett, the treasurer. Many local tradesmen gave their time and materials to redecorate the house including Mr Angelinetta, Mr Easley, Mr Walker, Mr H Trow, Mr J Trow, Mr G Riddick, Mr Maslin, Mr W Chequer, and Ernest James Lansdown of 53 High Street. Others gave their time to clean the house from top to bottom. Many residents offered items of furniture.

Although we do not know how Wootton Bassett's refugees were chosen, it must have been similar to the procedure documented in Purton. A representative from the town probably travelled up to Earl's Court, London, to meet Mrs Arnold-Forster, select a suitable family, and set a date to transport the family down to Wootton Bassett. Wootton Bassett welcomed their Belgian refugees to the town on November 2nd 1914. They were the Van Rickstal family from Antwerp.[7]

A second Belgian group, a Miss and Mrs de Winter, who were nurses from Ambulance Number 72, Antwerp, and the Stas family from Esterbecq, a suburb of Antwerp, arrived in the High Street later that month. The De Winters immediately placed an advertisement in a column in 'De Belgische Koerier' ('The Belgian Courier') where people could appeal for help in finding lost compatriots. They were seeking the whereabouts of some Belgian soldiers, Eugene Bastogne, Pierre Clerebout, Gustave Paridaens, Prosper Beckman, 1st Chef (Captain) Jean Ducerf and 1st Chef Blondeau.

Events in aid of the fund continued with unabated enthusiasm. On November 7th 1914 a football match was played in the Close, kindly lent by Mr Drury. The match was between Wootton Bassett and the South Western Mounted Brigade Field Ambulance Royal Army Medical Corps, based in Swindon. The Wootton Bassett team consisted of Beasley, Joseph Cannon, Watts, Kembrey, Boulter, Bull, Leighfield, Dixon, Watts, Lawes, and Flewelling (no first names are given). Mr E Wallis was the referee. A pleasant game resulted in a three-nil victory for the Royal Army Medical Corps. The Town Band provided entertainment, and in the evening a smoking concert was held at the Red Lion Assembly Rooms, with Howard Horsell

---

[7] For the Van Rickstal's story see 164 High Street in the Town companion volume.

presiding, and a selection of songs with Miss King at the piano. The gate receipts for the match, £1 8s 11d, and the proceeds of the concert, about £1 10s, were donated to the Belgian Refugee fund.

An evening concert in aid of the fund took place in the Council Schools on the 26th November 1914, before a packed and supportive audience. The musicians were a party of ladies and gentlemen from Swindon comprising Miss May Burley soprano, Mr W F Church tenor, Mr Ken Ellis bass, Mr W H Wood humorist, Miss Kathleen Ainsworth elocutionist, Mr W H Baker violinist, and Miss Irene Jones solo pianist and accompanist. Mr Seth Perkins, violinist, was prevented from being present through 'severe indisposition', but Mr Barker, at the very last moment, consented to take his place. The excellent programme was so appreciated by the crowded audience that they demanded repeated encores. At the close of the concert, Frank Bartlett proposed a hearty vote of thanks to their Swindon friends for their kindness, and for their excellent programme. The evening concluded with a rendition of the National Anthem.

In the Petty Sessions on Saturday, 13th February 1915, Mr Robert Little, overseer, applied on behalf of the Belgian Relief Committee to be excused from the payment of rates in respect of the houses where the refugees were living. Mr Little told Admiral Wilson that there were two such houses in the High Street. The application was granted but regrettably the address of the second house, presumably that occupied by the de Winter and the Stas family, was not recorded.

Wootton Bassett's Belgian families were invited to join a party of Belgians from Swindon, Highworth, and Purton as the guests of Mrs Arnold-Forster at Basset Down on Saturday, 10th July 1915. The 200 guests, including committee members, made their way to the house in an impressive fleet of motor cars loaned by a variety of residents and businesses including the Southern Laundry, the Rifleman's Hotel, Dr

Moore, Mr Barnard, Miss Deacon, Mr Balch, Mr George, Edward Hiscock, Mr Morley, Mrs Calley, Mrs Currie from Aldbourne, three cars from Mr Skurray of Skurrays garage in Swindon, Mr Crowdy, Mrs Lavery, Mrs Rattray, Mr Griffiths, Mr English, and Mr Bowly. The weather was fine, and the group very much enjoyed the tea which was laid on for them. There was a 'pretty entertainment' given by some of the Belgian children under the direction of Madame Stas and Mlle Vanderneyden. The little ones were quaintly dressed in a variety of costumes and gave an excellent performance. After the show, the guests promenaded around the grounds of Basset Down. At the end of the afternoon, Monsieur Tamboise thanked Mrs Arnold-Forster and Mrs Story Maskelyne for their hospitality on behalf of all the guests.

A particularly entertaining concert in aid of the Belgian Relief Fund was held at the Council Schools on Thursday, 7th December 1916. There was a fairly large audience, and the performers were 'The Wags' from Swindon. Mr Richardson and Mr Wood lifted everyone's spirits with performances which were described as 'screamingly funny', including a song entitled 'When Maud put her new bathing costume on'. After expenses, the concert raised over £5.

A very successful 'Khaki Concert' in aid of the Fund was held at the Council Schools on Wednesday evening, January 16th 1918. The concert was arranged by Mrs H Perry of Swindon assisted by her daughter, Kathleen Perry. The performers were soldiers from Chiseldon Camp, who attended with the kind permission of Lieutenant Colonel G E Pyle, together with 'The Specks' troupe. The programme was light and contained many comic songs and duets. The performers included Drummer T Watts pianist, Sergeant A Spurden singer, Private S G Bonser singer, Master Leslie Speck singer, Private R Teale singer, and Sergeant E Miles, singer. Kathleen Perry sang 'La

Belle Parisienne', and Bandsman W Wilman performed an instrumental speciality. Despite the inclement weather, there was a large and enthusiastic audience, who greeted the performances with unstinting applause and frequent encores. The programme closed with a speech of thanks from Daniel Kembrey.

The Soldiers and Sailors Families Association (SSFA)

The Soldiers and Sailors Families Association (SSFA) was founded in 1885, and when war broke out, it was the only national Service charity in existence. After the formation of the Royal Air Force in 1918, the Soldiers and Sailors Families Association became the Soldiers Sailors and Airmen's Families Association. In 1914 the association recruited 50,000 volunteers to carry out their work. The local division of the Soldiers and Sailors Families Association was the Cricklade Division (737) which was based in Purton. The Chairman was Miss Warrender of Stoke House, Purton, Wootton Bassett's representative was Mrs Little of the High Street, Lydiard Tregoze and Lydiard Millicent were represented by Miss Story Maskelyne, Lyneham and Tockenham were represented by Mrs Twine, and Broad Town was represented by Reverend L Cawker. In 1914 alone, SSFA volunteers helped over one million Forces family members across the UK and Ireland. In the Cricklade division grants of £61 17s were made during 1914 in support of 28 wives, 91 children, and 12 other relatives.

Local Relief Funds

At the beginning of August 1914, the War Office warned that measures should be taken to prepare for all kinds of difficulties, including unemployment, food shortages, price increases, disorder, and financial suffering. The National Relief Fund, with the Prince of Wales as its principal, was founded on August 7th 1914, and within 24 hours it had raised over £250,000. In Wootton Bassett, relief was available to the dependants of serving men from The Soldiers' and Sailors' Families Association and the Red Cross, both of which were represented in the parish, but there was nothing in place to assist those affected by the war in other ways. Towards the end of September, at the instigation of the Rural District Council, the Parish Council determined to create a formal Local Relief Committee to deal with any cases of distress arising through the war, other than those of dependants. The Parish Council agreed to act as a temporary committee, joined by John Boulter of 5 Church Street and George Mitchell of 29 Church Street as representatives of the railwaymen. At the first meeting at the Town Hall on the 29th September 1914, a committee of 22 was formally appointed including the seventeen members of the Council who had already volunteered themselves, and five additional members: Reverend Mathias, Howard Horsell, Richard Tom Tayler from Bank House, and grocers Henry Weston of 156 High Street, and Charles Edward Street of 155 High Street. It was decided that the committee would meet regularly in the Parish Office and that the members would make a collection in the parish without delay. Howard Horsell immediately offered £2 to launch the fund.

At the annual Parish Meeting in March 1918 the Parish Council proposed a central scheme for raising funds for all war relief charities, excluding the Prisoners of War Fund, which would continue to be catered for separately. The principle was that anyone could contribute money or gifts in kind, which could either be earmarked for a particular cause, or could be used as the committee thought fit if no cause was specified. It was proposed to invite the neighbouring parishes in the Cricklade and Wootton Bassett Union to join in with this scheme.

Something to Smoke

Relief comes in many forms. The soldiers and sailors of the Great War used smoking to help them relax, cope with boredom and undoubtedly to relieve stress. A 1915 poster for the Sailors' and Soldiers' Tobacco Fund designed by Frank Brangwyn ARA stated:

It is a significant fact that almost every letter from the front contains a request for 'something to smoke'.

In the Swindon area, the baton was taken up by the North Wilts Herald who ran many adverts appealing for donations to their Tobacco Fund. The newspaper explained their mission:

Every sixpence contributed to our Tobacco Fund helps to bring a ray of sunshine into the lives of the brave boys who are serving their King and country, and we feel sure that the appeal we are making to the generosity of the thousands of readers of the North Wilts Herald will not be in vain. After a hard day's work in the trenches, there is nothing that our 'Tommies' enjoy so much as a smoke.

Local sympathy and support for this fund arose immediately. At the end of the first meeting of the National Relief Fund's local committee in August 1914, Henry Weston made a collection for the purpose of providing the men of the Wiltshire Regiment at the front with tobacco. Fundraising continued throughout the war. Richard Parsons of Hunt Mill was among the Wootton Bassett worthies who contributed to the North Wilts Herald Tobacco Fund. His donation of 5 shillings was acknowledged in the paper on 7th January 1916.

National Egg Collection

In December 1914 a nationwide National Egg Collection appeal was launched, administered by a Committee based at Fleet Street, London. They aimed to collect 200,000 eggs per week for the wounded. By April 1915 the Society was achieving 170,000 eggs per week. Poultry farmers could despatch the eggs to the central London depot free of rail costs, or to one of the 2,000 local depots across the UK, and the eggs were distributed on from these to the hospitals in Britain and abroad, by the war office. As far as possible, egg boxes were returned to the farmers for re-use. People who had their own chickens were asked to give a proportion of their eggs each week. Those without chickens were encouraged to give money so that eggs could be bought. At the end of July 1915, Queen Alexandra became the patron of the scheme, and on August 16th the collection was given renewed impetus through her Alexandra Week, aiming to double collection from 500,000 to 1,000,000.

Mrs T Arkell was the president of the local branch of National Egg Collection for the Wounded, based in Stratton, Swindon. In total, the branch collected 161,651 eggs, the eleventh highest of 2,000 depots nationally. By January 1918 the scheme had sent over seven million eggs to hospitals at home and over 25 million to hospitals abroad. Many of the eggs were sent marked up with names or addresses on them, and some of these produced delightful stories. In W D Bavin's book "Swindon's War Record" a lovely tale is told of a donated egg which found its way to a Clyffe Pypard man in a French hospital.

Thomas Tucker, known as Tommy, was born in Purton Workhouse to a 19-year-old single mother, Elizabeth Tucker, who died a few weeks later. He was brought up for a few weeks by a Mrs Eacott, who may have been a wet nurse. He was then raised by William and Sarah Comley in Clyffe Street, in the village of Clyffe Pypard. By 1901 Sarah was widowed and worked as the caretaker of the village church. By this time Tommy was a farm labourer. He soon joined the 1st Wiltshire Regiment (5859) and served in the Boer War in South Africa. He had not returned home by the time war broke out and had lost touch with his guardian, Sarah. In 1914 Tommy would have been called up as a serving soldier or a reservist. He was a Private and went out to France on the 12th of September 1914, where he was wounded. W D Bavin takes up the story of the eggs:

Hundreds of letters of appreciation were received by the donors and officials, one of the most noteworthy being received by a little girl of Kingsdown. Her egg went from an egg-service held at St Philip's Church, Upper Stratton, to a hospital in France, and was given to a sick lad who had left Swindon ten years before, and who had been lost to his parents, all efforts to trace him having been vain. A letter received by Mrs Sellers ran as follows: - "Dear Madam, In the battle of ... (sic) I had the misfortune to be shot through the head; I was taken to hospital, and after being made comfortable in bed my first meal consisted of an egg bearing your address, and as I come from Wootton Bassett I thought I must write and thank you for it. I wish you could see the joy on the poor fellows' faces when they get the eggs; it would fully repay you for all your trouble. Again thanking you, Yours truly, T Tucker."

On 23 Nov 1917, Tom was discharged with a Silver War Badge, declared no longer physically fit for war service. He was awarded the Victory Medal, the British War Medal, and the 1914 Star. Tom went to work for Mr Davis in Bushton and stayed with the family for several years. (Mr Davis' daughter Elizabeth later married Charlie Tayler from the Angel). Tom married Edith Pile in 1921, and they had four children, Charles, Ida, Dorothy and Kate. He is listed on the Clyffe Pypard Roll of Honour.

Fig 6 - Tommy Tucker, with thanks to the Tucker family.

The First Casualties

The North Wilts Herald published their first full list of casualties, both killed and wounded, on October 9th 1914. No Wootton Bassett men were listed; nevertheless, the impact of the war locally could not have been lost on the parishioners of Wootton Bassett. Each death, falling ever closer on the heels of the last, brought grief and heartbreak, and must have struck cold fear into the hearts of mothers, wives, and girlfriends throughout the town.

Prisoners of War

The following men from the Wootton Bassett area were taken prisoner, some in the first month of the war. Their stories are told in the two companion volumes.

- Reginald Beacham
- Frank Sly
- Albert James Curtis
- Arthur Beazley (died in captivity)
- Wilfred George Taylor
- Clarence Henry Leighfield
- Edmund Eggleston
- Alfred John Embling
- Lewington Harold Weare
- Howard James Smart
- John Pickett Spackman (killed in captivity)
- Maurice William Reeves
- William Henry Bint (died in captivity)
- F Merrett
- Victor Charles Lansdown
- H Drury

- W Titcombe

In November 1914 news arrived that two of the town's young men, Corporal Reginald Beacham and Corporal Frank Sly, had become prisoners of war. Later, Corporal Albert James Curtis was taken prisoner. Reginald, Frank and Albert must have known each other well, as for a time all three families lived in Wood Street.

In Swindon, a public appeal was launched in October 1914 for funds to provide the men serving on the front with woollen mittens, scarves, cardigans, socks, and other requisites. For many months thereafter the ladies' committee which administered this scheme also took on the task of forwarding bread and other provisions to the men of the Wiltshire Regiment who were prisoners of war in Germany. By the end of 1915, they were supporting over 600 Wiltshire POWs interned in 19 different camps. Many other novel means were found to support the prisoners. The Swindon Bootmakers' Society, for example, undertook to repair boots for them free of charge. In many cases, parents and friends of prisoners personally sent parcels to the prison camps, but a more equitable solution was sought, particularly given that the families of prisoners often struggled to provide for their loved ones. The Wiltshire Prisoners of War Fund fulfilled this demand.

The Wiltshire Prisoners of War Fund was in full swing by 1916. Money for the fund was raised through donations of all kinds, as well as regular collections from local tradesmen and collections. The Wiltshire committee took pride in the fact that they could trace every parcel sent, and they received many letters of gratitude from prisoners who had received the parcels. By February 1917 the County committee at Trowbridge was decreeing regional and parish targets for fundraising, which were expected to be met by a voluntary rate of 3d in the pound, or a house to house collection. The idea of the voluntary rate caused much controversy. Some parishes agreed immediately, including Clyffe

Pypard, which met its quota immediately, as well as Latton, Braydon, Lydiard Millicent, Lydiard Tregoze, Marston Maisey, Lyneham, Purton, Tockenham and Broad Town. Others agreed to do their best to raise what they could, including Leigh and Cricklade. Ashton Keynes refused absolutely to participate in the scheme.

Wootton Bassett Parish Council discussed the matter in March 1917, with some members expressing their regret at the apparent indifference to the pathetic appeal of 700 men who had faced death for those at home, and who were now enduring captivity among ruthless enemies. They concluded that in principle they should make every effort to meet the targets, but they had some reservations concerning the general concept of a voluntary rate and that those who would be required to pay should have a say in the matter. Eventually, it was agreed that the local Red Cross Committee should be invited to organise a canvas of the parish for voluntary contributions instead. Collections continued throughout the war. Late in November 1917, the Red Cross Working Party was asked to arrange an additional collection for the Wiltshire Prisoners of War Fund throughout the parish, as the quota due was considerably behind. In July 1918 Mr A Boyce was appointed as the treasurer of the local Prisoners of War Fund in place of bank manager Richard Tom Tayler who had left the parish.

The death of Lord Roberts

During the war years, it appears that the death of any national hero had a significant impact on morale, even at a local level. The death of Field Marshal Frederick Sleigh Roberts, 1st Earl Roberts, was a particular sorrow to the local community, not least due to his association with Reverend Mathias, whose father in law had served under Lord Roberts, as colonel of a native regiment, throughout the Afghan War. At the Parish Church on the following evening, Reverend

Mathias spoke with feeling about the life of Lord Roberts, which had been spent entirely in the service of his country. At the end of the service the organist, William Timbrell Baxter, played Handel's Dead March from Saul, and on the next Thursday evening, a muffled peal was rung on the church bells in Lord Roberts' honour. This is the first reference I have found to the playing of the Dead March during the war, but, along with Chopin's infamous Marche Funebre, it was to be repeated many times at funerals and remembrance services throughout the war.

Nursing and The Red Cross

There were eighteen Voluntary Aid Detachments in the county of Wiltshire by March 1914, but Wootton Bassett was not among them and did not acquire its own detachment until long after the war, in 1928. However, the Swindon and North Wilts Division of the Red Cross Society was already well established at the Technical School in Swindon when war broke out. The President was Colonel Calley's wife Emily Calley, the secretary was Mrs W L Waugh of Burderop Park, and the Treasurer was Mr W G Little. Many men and women had already qualified in First Aid and Home Nursing at the Technical School, and nearly all the qualified nurses in Swindon immediately offered their services to the Red Cross. New classes were arranged to meet both the rising demand from local folk anxious to help and to answer the nation's call for more qualified nurses.

The Auxiliary Military Hospitals were operated by the Red Cross under their Voluntary Aid Detachments, so again, there were none in Wootton Bassett. By October 1914 the Red Cross had converted the swimming baths in Swindon into a temporary hospital for sick Territorials from the new military camp near Chiseldon. The initial inmates were those who, according to the local paper, were not yet hardened to campaigning and had been taken ill with minor ailments. Many local ladies who had taken courses in first aid and home nursing volunteered to help at the hospital, and this may well have included some from Wootton Bassett. The other nearby hospitals were Bowood in Calne, Pavilion in Calne, Charlton Park near Malmesbury, Marlborough, Cirencester and Melksham. Red Cross hospitals were also opened in Chippenham at the Town Hall in November 1915 the Neeld in August 1916. Wiltshire, as a whole, served a remarkable 3,379 military patients by June 30th 1915, in a period of less than a year. In contrast to this activity within the county, very few Red Cross staff from Wiltshire went abroad. On 30th June 1915, 19 women and 10 men of the Wiltshire detachments were working in full military hospitals or in France.

The Wootton Bassett and Cricklade Board of Guardians met in September 1916 to consider the possibility that the Government might require the workhouse premises for the care of wounded soldiers. The Chairman remarked that this would be an economical move as the workhouse was only half full. The Medical Officer had indicated that provision could easily be made for a hundred beds. A resolution was carried in support of any such proposal, although Mr Tuck said that whilst he did not wish to go so far as to vote against the resolution, he was not so sure that a workhouse was a nice place for wounded soldiers, especially as there were much better places in the district that might be used in preference. He suggested that there was a place in Wootton Bassett and another in Purton that might be made available for the care of wounded men. Regrettably, the Herald does not record the addresses of these alternatives. I have found no evidence that wounded servicemen were ever cared for in the town.

Although there was no local hospital in Wootton Bassett, the Red Cross developed a strong and confident presence in the town. On Monday 10th August 1914, less than a week after war was declared, a crowded meeting was held at the Town Hall, with Mrs Buxton from Tockenham Manor in the chair. It was decided to form a Red Cross fundraising group, a Working Party to make garments and other hospital requisites, and an Ambulance group.[8] A ladies' committee was formed, and it was decided that they would meet once a week.

---

[8] The name Ambulance seems to have been used interchangeably with First Aid, to describe initial medical care, for example, the Scouts had Ambulance competitions to demonstrate their first aid skills.

First Aid Training (Ambulance) and Nursing

A number of Wootton Bassett residents qualified in First Aid in an examination held on October 5th 1914: The lecturer was Doctor Bogle, and the examiner was Doctor F Lewarne of Cricklade. The successful candidates were:

- Miss Agnes Ruth Bevir (no VAD record identified)
- Miss Gwendoline Maud Bond, 57 High Street, Red Cross nurse
- Miss Catherine Church, 1 Wood Street and 149 High Street
- Miss E Clifford, not identified
- Miss Lilly Edwards, housemaid at Upper Woodshaw Farm
- Miss Lucy Humphries, Red Cross nurse, see 56 High Street and the Red Cross Legacy
- Mrs A H Hunt, not identified
- Mr F Hunt, not identified
- Miss Emilie Mathias, The Vicarage, Station Road
- Mrs Julie Morgan, 28 Wood Street, Red Cross nurse
- Mrs Hilda Triffie Ray, 149 High Street (no VAD record identified)
- Mrs Louisa Wallis, 1 Coxstalls (no VAD record identified)
- Miss Alison Weston, 156 High Street
- Miss Witt, not identified.

In 1915 the British Red Cross Association held a series of nursing classes in the Red Lion Assembly Rooms courtesy of Mr and Mrs Pearce. There were 26 attendees, 18 of whom entered an examination at the Council Schools on December 21st. The lecturer was Miss Prescott of the Portland Nursing Home, Bath, and the examiner was the town doctor, Dr Watson. Certificates were awarded to:

- Miss Agnes Ruth Bevir (as in 1914 above)
- Miss Gwendoline Maud Bond (as in 1914 above)
- Miss Catherine Church (as in 1914 above)
- Miss F M Clifford
- Mrs Laura Cotton, 68 High Street
- Miss G P Curtis, possibly Grace Theodocia Gentilla Charlotte of 166 High Street but middle initial incorrect
- Miss Lilly Edwards (as in 1914 above)
- Miss Florence Mary Hart, 4 Wood Street
- Miss Lucy Humphries (as in 1914 above)
- Mrs M L G Hunt
- Miss H E Hunter, not identified
- Miss Emilie Mathias (as in 1914 above)
- Mrs T Morgan, not identified
- Mrs Lizzie Meana Newth, 54 High Street, (no VAD record identified)
- Mrs F R Newton, not identified
- Mrs Hilda Triffie Ray (as in 1914 above)
- Mrs Louisa Wallis (as in 1914 above)
- Miss Alison Weston (as in 1914 above).

Red Cross Fundraising

The local committee started collecting funds for the Red Cross during the very first week of the war and maintained their support steadfastly throughout the war. In October every year from 1915 onwards, Wootton Bassett participated in the national collection drive for the Red Cross and the Order of St John, known as "Our Day". All the collectors were women and young ladies of the town, and each one was allocated a street or streets where they would sell flags. Many of the ladies were out and about from early in the morning until late in the day. In 1915 "Our Day" raised £19.15s and in 1916 it raised £15.2s. In May 1915 the town participated in an appeal for the St John Ambulance Association and the Red Cross Society Penny Fund for Sick and Wounded. The local president was Colonel Calley's wife, Mrs Calley, and the honorary secretary was Mrs Swinhoe. The Wootton Bassett collectors were Miss Church, Miss Hart, Mrs Hunt, C Hawkes, Lily Lawrence and Miss Watts. The six collectors contributed 13s.1d towards the total amount raised, which was over £38. Miniature Russian flags were sold by a number of ladies in the town on Saturday, September 17th 1915, on behalf of the Russian Red Cross. It was another successful appeal, with excellent work carried out by the collectors.

Local farmers established their own group to raise funds for the British Farmers' Red Cross Fund. In August 1915 Messrs Armstrong and Son, auctioneers, appealed for donations for the auction they planned to hold on behalf of the British Farmers' Red Cross Fund, (although donors could specify other funds to which the proceeds of their lots could be given if they so wished). The Fund had already equipped and despatched two hospitals, costing £10,000, to Serbia, contributed to Dr Barrie's hospital in Serbia, King George's Hospital London, and an enteric hospital in Calais, France, and had bought five Red Cross motor lorries. Supporters were now aiming to raise £100,000 for the Red Cross, in order to provide accommodation for troops in Malta and to supply a convoy of motor ambulances. The auction was to take place after the usual market sales on the following Wednesday. It was advertised locally, with free printing by Mr Riddick and free billposting by Mr Joseph Wiltshire, with no further touting or wider canvassing. The auction was to include livestock, poultry, eggs, implements, furniture, potatoes and other garden and farm produce. Local patrons included Howard Horsell of Wootton Bassett, William Hosier of

Queen Court Farm, Tockenham, Edward Hiscock of Lydiard Park, Henry Manners of Cotmarsh, R Parsons of Hunt Mill, J Price of Broad Town, W H Rabbetts of Broad Town, E J Tuck of Broad Town, J Spackman of Clyffe Pypard, A R Strange of Wootton Bassett, and H White of Midgehall. The sale was a complete success, and achieved over £126, with further donations expected afterwards. As the Herald reported, "the farmers, tradesmen and labourers in the Wootton Bassett district know how to give when the object appeals to their patriotism and sense of duty." The success of the sale was largely thanks to the energy and persistence displayed by Messrs W Drury, H White and others, who made things lively by frequently buying goods and then immediately donating the goods back to the Auctioneers to be resold, and inducing others to do the same. A fat lamb given by Hervey William White was sold and resold no less than 69 times, resulting in an aggregate of over £44. A dozen eggs were sold and resold 8 times resulting in proceeds of 14s 6d.

On September 1st 1915 a further sale was held at Wootton Bassett Market in support of the fund. The sale raised £130.7s, and this was forwarded to the Headquarters at Tower Bridge Mills, London. Messrs Armstrong and Son also held a jumble sale in Wootton Bassett in October 1915 and afterwards donated £100 of their takings to the fund. It must have been very high-class jumble, as this would represent over £8000 in today's money.

One noteworthy sale held by Messrs Armstrong for the British Farmers' Red Cross Fund took place in the Market Place on June 6th 1917. The sale began with the usual full inventory auction, with plenty of stock in all departments including implements and farm vehicles. After this there was a special entry of 22 fowl donated by Miss Twine of the Manor House, to be sold in aid of the British Farmers' Red Cross Fund. The fowl raised an amount entirely disproportionate to their value, and this was largely due to the splendid efforts of Hervey William White and the Twine brothers, who bought, donated and resold the birds several times over and induced others to follow their patriotic example. The final total raised from the sale of the fowl was the extraordinary sum of £16 5s 6d, well over £1000 in today's money.

The Red Cross Working Party

The first meeting of the Working Party was held at the Red Lion Assembly Room on August 13th 1914. Its goal was to support the work of the Red Cross, under the direction of the Swindon and North Wilts Division. An advertisement placed by the Division in the North Wilts Herald of August 15th 1914 gives a good summary of its requirements. The article read:

The work of the above Society is now being rapidly organised in this District. Everyone can help. Offers of help are needed as follows:
1) For Needlework of all kinds.
2) Convalescent homes for sick and wounded.
3) Services of those men and women who have BOTH First Aid and Home Nursing Certificates for Staff of temporary Hospitals.
4) Cooks, who can do invalid cooking and cooking for staff.
5) To lend beds, bedding, etc., for temporary rest stations.
6) Gifts of money, which should be sent to the Hon. Secretary.
Those willing to help in the Wootton Bassett district were invited to apply to Mrs Buxton of Tockenham Manor or Mrs Watson in Wootton Bassett.

At the first meeting some 120 items were given out, (it is unclear what these were, but possibly they were needlework materials for sewing), and a meeting was scheduled for the following Thursday.

The Red Cross continued its work in Wootton Bassett under the direction of the Swindon branch throughout 1914. They achieved a great deal, particularly for such a small town without the incentive of a hospital of its own. By December the town had raised £30 from individual subscriptions and from collections at the Church and the Brotherhood. The Working Party had held fifteen meetings in the Red Lion's Assembly Room, kindly lent by Mr and Mrs Pearce. The group had sewn and knitted numerous articles to be sent to the soldiers using materials donated by Mrs Bevir, Mrs Fernie and Mrs Dale. This included sixteen pairs of pyjamas, 21 pairs of bed socks, 27 pairs of day socks, four pairs of sheets, 36 day flannel shirts, 23 nightshirts, seventeen vests, 33 bed jackets, 27 cholera belts, eleven kit bags, 46 huckaback towels, 28 bath towels, 36 handkerchiefs, 487 swabs, and 137 bandages. Further donations had arrived from individual ladies in the town including six pairs of day socks knitted by Mrs Cook, a pair of night socks knitted by Miss Corp, two pairs of day socks from Mrs Thompson and three dozen handkerchiefs from Mrs Florence Tayler, the bank manager's wife. The group appealed for more funds to buy material, and various members of the group, mainly unmarried young ladies, were encouraged to solicit donations, among them Miss Chequer, Miss Hunt, Miss Wallis, Miss Drury, Miss Marchant, Miss Smith, Miss Watkins, Miss Bond, Miss Weston, Mrs Florence Tayler, Miss Lucy Humphries, Miss MacFarlane, Miss Bevir and the most successful collector, Mrs Bevan, who single-handedly raised £9.17s.3d. The monies were administered by Mr Little.

By December 1915 helpers in Wootton Bassett had made more than 1030 articles and forwarded them to the Red Cross Society. Anxious to do more, the committee, comprising Mrs Bevan, Mrs Dale, Mrs Fernie, Mr Little, Miss Mathias, Miss A Mills, Mrs Florence Tayler, and Mrs Watson, launched a branch work party depot to supply surgical dressings and garments for the wounded. Weekly meetings were scheduled from December 1915 in the Parish Office. The Committee invited volunteers to attend weekly, fortnightly, or even just occasionally. As the depot was to be supported by donations, the committee also advertised for voluntary contributions towards materials. In February 1916 the Wootton Bassett Red Cross Society announced that they had held eight work parties in the Parish Room on Wednesdays, through which they had been able to send 268 articles to the Royal Academy, London. The items included bed-jackets, felt shoes, scultetus bandages (many-tailed), slings, washing face cloths, dusters, cushions, and various kinds of swabs. The local committee advertised that they would be glad to have more helpers.

In April 1919, having received notice from the Red Cross Headquarters that the time had come to disband, the voluntary Red Cross Working Party closed and its audited balance sheet was put on display in the window of the Parish Office. Since the beginning of the war, the Red Cross had achieved a great deal. It had received £90 in donations, but the collection of donations paled into insignificance compared to the effort which had been put into the collection, sewing and knitting of items for the wounded, and to give comfort to members of the armed forces. The impressive and carefully itemised inventory included 119 pairs of pyjamas, 48 pairs of bed-socks, four pairs of sheets, 92 day shirts, 37 nightshirts, 95 vests, 57 bed jackets, 27 cholera belts, eleven kit-bags, 46 huckaback towels, 28 bath towels, 36 handkerchiefs, 637 swabs, 338 bandages, 86 pairs of pants, 24 pairs of felt slippers, seven pairs of operation socks, three pairs of day socks, one pair of gloves, 57 mufflers, 170 face cloths, nineteen dusters, 67 cushions with covers, nine pairs of mittens, 30 slings, 57 fly covers, 45 comfort bags, 25 pillow slips, and two feather pillows. In addition, thanks to donations of material, 230 bags had been sent to Mrs Napier Miles for Lady Smith-Dorrien's Hospital Bag Fund. Olive Smith-Dorrien was the wife of General Sir Horace Lockwood Smith-Dorrien. Hearing that wounded soldiers were often separated from their personal effects and valuables while in hospital, she rallied women around the country to sew so-called comfort bags. Volunteers nationwide sewed over 40,000 bags a month, totalling about five million throughout the war. For this work, she was created a Dame Commander of the Order of the British Empire (DBE).

The Red Cross medal was instituted in 1920 and was awarded to members who had undertaken at least 1,000 hours of unpaid service or had been ambulance drivers and bearers who gave 500 hours unpaid service. Between 41,000 and 42,000 were awarded, which gives some idea of the immense operation the Red Cross undertook in the war, and the incredible commitment of the women of Britain. I have not identified any recipients from Wootton Bassett.

The Red Cross Legacy

After the closure of the Working Party in 1919 there was no formal Red Cross presence in the town until 1928 when Julie Morgan opened the town's first Red Cross Detachment.[9] After her death in 1929, she was succeeded as Commandant by Lucy Humphries.

Humphries, Lucy Elizabeth

Lucy Humphries lived at Fairview, 56 High Street. She took part in the first aid training classes organised in Wootton Bassett. She went on to volunteer as a nurse at Westbury, Trowbridge, and Bowood House Hospitals in Wiltshire, for seven months full time between 1916 and 1918. Lucy Dixon (see below) felt sure that Lucy Humphries was awarded the Red Cross medal for her duties in the war, but this was not confirmed by Lucy Humphries' VAD membership card, and her seven months' work would not have qualified her for the medal. She may have earned the medal after the war, however. Lucy was not only active in the Red Cross, but also in fundraising, and supporting the

---

[9] For Julie Morgan's story see 28 Wood Street in the Town companion volume.

Boy Scouts. She was well known for the fabulous range of entertainments and pageants she organised and contributed to, and there are many references to her throughout these pages. For many years after the war, Red Cross meetings were held in the upstairs room of the coach house at Fairview. Lucy Humphries was Commandant until at least 1944. She never married and died at Fairview in 1958.

Fig 7 - The Red Cross members in the garden of Fairview in the High Street, with thanks to Lucy Dixon

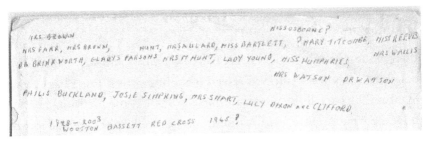

Fig 8 - Key to photograph of The Red Cross members, with thanks to Lucy Dixon

Hunt, Maud

The next Commandant was Lucy Humphries' former Assistant, Maud L C Hunt. Maud lived in Old Court and had two children, Peggy and Gordon. After Lucy Humphries' death in 1958 the Red Cross meetings were moved from pillar to post depending on what premises were available, including church halls and even upstairs in pubs. In the late 1960s general meetings, lectures, first aid training and nursing training were held at Wootton Hall, which had previously belonged to Lucy Humphries and now belonged to the British Legion.

Parsons, Gladys Asenath

Miss Gladys Asenath Parsons, who was born in 1902 and was probably a founder member of the branch, had become the Assistant Commandant by 1955. She became the Commandant in 1956. Gladys resigned in 1968.

Fig 9 - Long service awards awarded in 1968, with thanks to Lucy Dixon. The photograph was taken in Wootton Hall, Sparrow Lane, in 1968. You can just see a portrait of Lucy Humphries in Red Cross uniform hanging on the wall between the ladies.

Dixon, Lucy

Lucy Humphries' gardener at Fairview, Mr Clifford, named his daughter Lucy Joan Clifford after Lucy Humphries. Lucy has always lived at 29 Coxstalls in Wootton Bassett. She left the National School, now the Civic Centre, on the afternoon before her 14th birthday, and immediately started work for E H and A S Hunt, the bakery and provisions shop, in Wootton Bassett High Street. Lucy grew up heavily involved in the Red Cross and was often called upon to act the part of a patient. She can remember attending meetings in the Coach House before World War II, in about 1938. She particularly recalls being wrapped in cotton wool, which was a treatment for pneumonia. She also remembers that during World War II, there was a dirty head clinic for evacuees in Wootton Hall and the Red Cross had to make sure both adults and children were free of lice. Lucy met her husband-to-be, Philip Leonard Dixon, known as Jim, when his jumper caught on her watch during a dance. They married in St Bartholomew's Church four years later, in 1952. Lucy and Philip had two sons, Keith and Philip junior. After many years of service, Lucy Dixon became the last Commandant of the Wootton Bassett branch.

Fig 10 - Lucy Dixon, with thanks to Lucy Dixon

Andrews, Sheila

Lucy's colleague Sheila Andrews lived in Station Road. She moved with her family from Ludgershall in 1938 and lived in Wootton Bassett for the rest of her life. She attended the National School (now the Civic Centre). She became a Red Cross cadet and later leader and centre organiser. She operated an independent service, Wootton Bassett Medical Loans, which provided short term use of items from walking sticks and bedpans to wheelchairs, and was the local contact for the Blood Donor service. She was noted for her kindness and unstinting service to others. During the Second World War Sheila was a volunteer with the National Hospital Service Reserve. She had to be ready to go to work anywhere in the country. Her first duty was helping evacuees from London who were escaping the blitz.

The Red Cross after WW2

The Red Cross branch remained active in the town throughout the post World War 2 years, acting under the direction of local GPs wherever the need arose. Volunteers regularly attended events such as amateur dramatic productions, the annual mayor's ball, the Broad Town Show, the Dickensian Night and High Street Festival, school fetes, gymkhanas as well events organised by a host of local groups including the Wootton Bassett Light Operatic Society and the Rugby Club. In 1971, Lucy Dixon and Sheila Andrews were invited to a garden party at Buckingham Palace attended by the Queen, Prince Philip and Princess Anne, in recognition of their service. Neither Lucy Dixon nor Sheila Andrews ever had to serve overseas, and they were told they were too old during the call up for the Falklands in 1982. But Lucy said that she still feels an affinity to volunteers working all around the world. She has always remembered with pride that the Red Cross doesn't take sides and cares for all people. During the 1970s Sheila

Andrews used to step in for nurses at the former Stratton St Margaret Hospital.

As the members grew older, the responsibility of the branch weighed heavier on Lucy and Sheila's shoulders. Lack of support and increasing bureaucracy made it unviable for it to continue. In 1999 Lucy was given a Civic Award for services to the town. She has received numerous commendations, including long service awards, from the Red Cross. By 2003 the group had dwindled to eight volunteers. Eventually at the end of 2003, after 75 years of service to the community, the branch closed. Lucy Dixon and Sheila Andrews received their Red Cross long service awards in 2003.

Sheila was 74 when the branch closed. She had been a Red Cross volunteer for 63 years. She said, "I decided to resign at the end of the year, and no-one else wished to take it over. The rest of my members decided to resign as well. I shall miss it, but there is no way we can carry on. We have tried all sorts of ways of encouraging new members. We lost our feeder when we lost the youth group two years ago. That was the beginning of the end. It has changed so much since I first joined. It has all got to do with insurance purposes. We need to give notice to the regional office six weeks in advance about any event we attend. We would offer our first-aid skills for free for any organisation that wanted us. If they wanted to give a donation to the Red Cross, that would be fine. But now all our duties have to be paid for. Obviously we don't get paid, but the money would go back to headquarters." Sheila died on 12th July 2010 and was buried in Wootton Bassett Cemetery. Sheila and her husband Roy, who died in 1960, had one son, Nigel, three grandchildren and two great-grandchildren.

Lucy Dixon was 77 when the branch closed. She had been a Red Cross volunteer for 65 years. She said: "Locally we are all really well-known.

We do a lot of jobs behind the scenes, not so much in uniform. Things like feeding, giving eye drops, dressing and bathing. But we can't do that any more down to new regulations. I have cared for people all my life, and I am sad the Red Cross is fading out in Wootton Bassett but I am not sad to be giving it up. My eyes are failing, and I am not as nimble as I used to be."

In 2005 The British Red Cross bought two units at Coped Hall, Wootton Bassett. The ground floor was to be a dedicated distribution centre to serve Wiltshire, Avon and Gloucestershire, and to store, maintain and clean the organisation's medical equipment. The first floor was to provide office space, a meeting centre and commercial and public training facilities, from a two hour 'Save a Life' course up to a full five-day training course. In addition, the British Red Cross planned to offer services from Coped Hall such as a 'home from hospital' service, transport and escort and services at public events. In April 2006 the commercial training arm of the British Red Cross moved into Coped Hall. In June 2006 the British Red Cross started looking for helpers for a new Medical Equipment Service operating from Coped Hall, loaning equipment such as wheelchairs to the public. Trained volunteers would be taking phone calls, issuing equipment to people and completing paperwork. The Red Cross moved out of the Coped Hall site in March 2019, bringing the Red Cross's presence in Wootton Bassett to a close.[10]

---

[10] My sincere thanks to Lucy Dixon for sharing her memories and pictures. Other information including Sheila Andrews' memories has been gleaned from the Gazette and Herald. For more information on the Red Cross, visit www.redcross.org.uk.

The War Years - 1915

As a new year dawned and the war was far from "over by Christmas", the mood in Wootton Bassett must have been a despondent one. January 3rd 1915 was appointed as a day of intercession on behalf of the Nation and Empire. At the Parish Church, the lessons were read by Robert Little and Reverend Mathias, and appropriate hymns were sung. William Timbrell Baxter concluded the service with a rendition of the Dead March from Saul. Some aspects of Wootton Bassett life went on much as usual. On the 6th January 1915, a market was held. The wet weather and flooding meant that the supply of stock was lower than usual, but prices were good, and trade was brisker than in other recent markets. Messrs Teagle and Sons sold over 30 head of cattle at the sale.

Recruitment

Wiltshire had done 'uncommonly well' in their recruitment for Kitchener's New Army, but as the North Wilts Herald reported in February 1915,

> ... there are still, both in town and country, many able-bodied young fellows who ought to be wearing the khaki and doing their bit for King and country, instead of idling away their time at whist drives, dances, picture palaces and the like; and it was with a view to getting hold of these 'slackers' and rousing them to a sense of their responsibility, that the military authorities hit upon the plan of organising a tour through the northern part of the county. What oratory has been unable to accomplish, the authorities seem to think that music and the spectacle of well-set-up young men wearing the King's uniform and swinging along to the strains of the band may possibly perform.

A party of soldiers from the 7th Battalion of the Wiltshire Regiment organised a recruitment march in February 1915. The tour party consisted of about 50 young men, who were at that time billeted in Marlborough. The tour was under the command of Lieutenant Sawtell and was accompanied by a recently formed band making excellent progress under the direction of Mr W R Patrick of Marlborough College. The men arrived at the Midland and South Western Junction Railway Station, off Newport Street in Swindon Old Town, on Tuesday. They marched to the top of Victoria Road, where the band struck up a lively tune. The soldiers wore red white and blue rosettes in their hats and looked exceedingly smart. From Swindon, they marched on to Purton, Cricklade, Malmesbury, Sherston, Crudwell, and Long Newnton.

On the morning of Saturday 27th February, the Regiment marched through Wootton Bassett. There was considerable excitement in town at their arrival. They had lunch at their billets in Wootton Bassett, then marched to Swindon for a football match. They returned to Wootton Bassett on the evening train, and the band gave a public concert in the Council Schools. Howard Horsell presided over a large audience, and the programme was much appreciated. Amongst those present were Alfred Ricks Humphries, Francis Teagle, and Henry Maslin, Captain Ennis, Sergeant Major Parfitt, Miss Lucy Humphries, Miss Bond, and M Bond. During the interval, Private Miller gave a stirring address and earnestly appealed to the young men to join them. Sergeant Major Parfitt asked the ladies present to aid the recruiting because the battle was being fought in the trenches in Flanders and France just as though the Germans were on British soil. He proposed a toast to Howard Horsell for presiding, and to Alfred Ricks Humphries for the use of the hall for the men during their stay in Wootton Bassett. The contingent left the town about 9.30 on Sunday morning, headed by their well-trained band, and accompanied by their new recruits, whose names, unfortunately, we do not know. They marched on to Calne and their final stop, Devizes.

At a meeting of the Rural District Council in August 1915, a letter was read from the recruiting officer Lieutenant Colonel Steward of Devizes inviting them to help with the canvassing of men eligible for the Army. They specifically suggested that those employed on this task should be men with tact, patience and ability to put the case clearly. The invitation met with a frosty reception. Mr Ward felt that the idea was misconceived and that it was an attempt to put onto civil shoulders what ought to be done by military authorities. They already had recruiting committees in the Rural District Council area and in Swindon, and these had already sent in the names of men who were eligible to serve, which would inevitably be supplemented by names from the official list. Civilians had been doing their utmost to induce young fellows to join the forces ever since the war began. There were, no doubt, a certain number of slackers, Mr Ward agreed, and others who could not quite make up their minds, but the work of roping them in should be in the hands of the recruiting sergeant, not civilians. He proposed replying to Lieutenant Colonel Steward to that effect and also suggested that the headquarters for recruiting in Wiltshire should be at Swindon, and not at Devizes.

Volunteer Training Corps

As the war progressed, men who were over military age or who were engaged in exempted occupations increasingly demanded a means to contribute to military life on the home front. There was no official group which they could join, so informal associations sprang up throughout the country to operate town guards and defence corps. On 19th November 1914, the Central Association of Volunteer Training Corps had been recognised by the War Office, and a Corps was quickly formed in Swindon, but it was not until May 1915 that Wootton Bassett answered the call for its own Corps. A meeting was held on the evening of Saturday, 29th May 1915 in order to form the Corps.

The meeting began with a stirring parade by the Swindon Volunteers. Immediately afterwards, a large group gathered at the Red Lion Assembly Room, with Howard Horsell presiding, assisted by Commandant T Robinson, Mr T Kimber and Mr W J Ainsworth from Swindon, and local gentlemen Edward Robert Case, Richard Parsons, E R Wallis and James Frank Underhill from the Post Office. Howard Horsell said that they were much indebted to their friends from Swindon who had marched down to assist them. He went on to speak of the present crisis, saying that England must look to itself to see that as many men as possible should be properly trained. He proclaimed:

We must never sheath the sword until those responsible for the atrocities recently perpetrated have been brought to justice. It is no time to find fault with the Government. You will all agree that the nation has done magnificently, and we must be a nation in arms. The National Reserve is a splendid movement, but the young men of England, knowing all they do, must do their part in this terrible struggle. Unless they do so, they are not worthy of the name of British subjects. It is quite possible for all men to give one evening a week for training. It is true that the average working man can not pay much, but if you have a smart drill-sergeant, there is no reason why Wootton Bassett should not produce a large number of trained men. I would be pleased to do all I can to assist, and by way of encouraging proficiency, I will offer 30 shillings in prizes and will place at your disposal the rifle range I opened some time ago for the use of the Scouts.

He also suggested that the lake might be used for swimming, which was very easy to learn. The Swindon Commandant, Mr T Robinson, agreed to send down a smart drill-instructor to help them, and he appealed to all to do their part. Howard Horsell then read an address given by Mr Hollister, who was the Mayor of Wootton Bassett in 1803 at the time of the threatened invasion of England by Napoleon. He read:

Gentlemen Volunteers - the Mayor of this borough addresses you as the servant and subject of his King and country to call on you your assistance when wanting in defence of this our kingdom now threatened by the prevailing constitution of France. Should the enemy obtain the wished-for effect, you and all true Britons must be made sacrifices to French ambition, such as plunder, massacre, debauchery and other diabolical mischief. Let us, my friends and Britons, come forward and volunteer our services in defence of our country and the constitution of old England, as prescribed by the several Acts of Parliament so to do. Our service will be doubly useful in case of necessity by being armed and instructed beforehand, and conducted by experienced officers approved by his Majesty King George the Third of the United Kingdom of Great Britain and Ireland. The service, it is hoped, will be short, under the assistance of our Almighty God, and there is the greatest hope and reason to believe that the knowledge of the hearts of all Englishmen, and their fighting the enemy, will be sufficient to prevent the enemy from putting the foot on the English shores to rob us of our lives and liberties. God save the King!

Mr Kimber then addressed the meeting and said that they wanted 50 men to form a platoon.

The present situation is very serious. For thousands of years, many nations have risen and fallen, and the issue we have to face today is: are we to remain a British Empire or come down? We are fighting a most powerful military nation, and we must beat them or go under. It is a great pity that so many young men with no ties will not join the Army, while so many married ones have gone out to fight their battles. This is not a time when the young man should shirk his duty. Many of you would be no use in the trenches, but there are many men who are willing to do the work that more able-bodied soldiers are doing at home and so relieve them for foreign service. It is a great crime for anyone to hesitate to do his duty.

Mr Ainsworth then explained the objects of the Volunteer Corps. He said:

There are many who hardly believe we are at war. They do not or will not realise that we are fighting a real war - the most terrible war in history. Every Englishman ought to do his part for his country now. The Army has called for all who are eligible for service, and those who are not eligible for the Army can help by joining the Volunteer Training Corps.

James Frank Underhill said that if ten other gentlemen gave two guineas each, he would be pleased to subscribe the same amount himself towards the funds of the Corps in Wootton Bassett. About twenty members were then enrolled. Mr Underhill said that the enrolment register could be kept at the Post Office so that any man who would like to join might register there at any time during the day.

Two months later the Herald reported that the Wootton Bassett Platoon of the Volunteer Training Corps was making excellent progress and now numbered 70 members. They had their first route march on Monday, 5th July 1915. On Sunday, 11th July 1915 they conducted a Church Parade through the town. They met at their headquarters under the command of George Marshall Watts and paraded with the town band at their head and the Boy Scouts in the rear. The service was conducted by the Reverend Fielding Daniels in locum tenens for the vicar, and it was said that he preached a stirring sermon. After the services, the Company paraded back through the town.

A social evening for the Wootton Bassett Volunteer Training Corps was held at the Red Lion Hotel on a Thursday evening in September 1915. Although the evening featured invited artistes and was essentially a recreational occasion, the Chairman took the opportunity to make a very stirring recruitment speech. Firstly he admonished those who had signed up with the Corps but thought it was acceptable to treat attendance at drill as optional or to resign without reasonable cause. This was, he said, a direct violation of the agreement they had entered into. He also pointed out that there were many able-bodied "slackers" who knew that the boys at the front were facing a foe who used asphyxiating gas and committed other atrocities contrary to the law of nations and worse than anything known since the Middle Ages. They were also perfectly aware that old men and women in France and Belgium had been murdered in cold blood and wives and daughters outraged. Unless the whole nation pulled together, there was a possibility that something similar would be brought to our own doors. He reminded the attendees that conscription would soon be upon them and that in the meantime, it was obvious that the vast majority of young fellows could give up an hour or two a week for military drill. He also stressed that after the war was over, people would be asking questions about the part they played in the greatest conflict the world had yet known. The meeting ended with a vote of thanks and the singing of the National Anthem.

Drills continued unabated. Weekly schedules for the Wootton Bassett Platoon of the Volunteers were listed in the North Wilts Herald. A typical week in November 1915 reads:

Sunday, November 14th, 2.45pm. - Meet at Assembly Room for
Church Parade at Brotherhood (Wood Street).
Monday, 7.30pm. - Platoon Drill.
Wednesday, 7.30pm. - NCOs Special Drill at Assembly Room
Thursday, 7.30pm. - Extended Order Drill.

Regular staff included Orderly Officer George Marshall Watts, Orderly Sergeant Henry Maslin, Orderly Corporal H C Francis,

Orderly Sergeant Edwin Helps, who was killed in action on 15th December 1916, and Orderly Corporal Frederick Barber, who later joined the Royal Army Medical Corps (74794) and served in France.

Howard Horsell had been providing some of his own land for a rifle range for the Scouts and the Volunteer Corps since at least May 1915. This may have been the rifle range marked on some old maps in the vicinity of The Lawns. By November he was seeking a more appropriate location for the range. At the Parish Council meeting on Wednesday, 24th November, the council considered an application from Mr Horsell for permission to use the piece of Council land abutting the Cemetery Lane as a miniature rifle range. The meeting could not make any decisions at that time due to the short notice, but the application was very favourably received. They were given to understand that War Office regulations would secure the erection of any barriers required for public protection in this much-frequented locality. It was resolved to lay the matter before the Parish Council at its next meeting, and it was duly raised on the agenda for Wednesday 21st April 1916. Despite the initial support for this idea, the proposal was now shelved due to lack of resources, and I have found no evidence that it was ever implemented.

Parades by the Volunteer Corps must have enlivened the streets of Wootton Bassett throughout the war. At a Church Parade for the Wootton Bassett section of the Volunteer Training Corps in December 1915, the Officer commanding was Mr Johnson, and Howard Horsell stood in as Orderly Officer. The Boy Scouts attended the parade with bugles and drums.

The Highlanders on Manoeuvres

The town was much excited in early July 1915 by the arrival of large numbers of men from the Seaforth Highlanders Regiment, who were stationed in Chiseldon, and were on manoeuvres in the area. As they passed through the town on Friday 2nd July 1915, about 5pm, one of the motor gun carriages which was proceeding up the High Street near the Town Hall collided with a motor car being driven by Lieutenant Adam Twine of Greenhill Common. The two soldiers who were accompanying the gun carriages were thrown off. One was badly scratched about the neck, but the other was virtually unharmed. First aid was rendered by two of the town's Red Cross ladies, Mrs Reeves and Miss Church, and the young soldiers were able to resume their journey, although both the gun carriage and the car were badly damaged.

National Defence Corps

A detachment of the National Defence Corps, another "Old Soldiers" organisation, headed by their bugles and drums, paraded through the High Street on Sunday, 14th November 1915. Unfortunately, their place of origin is unknown. After the parade, they attended a meeting of the Men's Own Brotherhood. Edward Henry Radbone presided, and Miss Hilda Knighton of Swindon was the soloist. An excellent address was given by Mr E N Tuck of Chippenham.

Trading Hours

Trading hours on the High Street during the war years were longer than we are used to today, and many shops remained open in the evenings, especially in the summer. A large number of tradesmen decided that from 10th May 1915 they would close their establishments daily from 1pm to 2pm (Saturday and Market Day excluded) in order to enjoy a regular midday meal. They respectfully asked for the kind cooperation of the public. Although no reason was given for this change, the War had probably reduced both the amount

[127]

of trade done by local businesses and the number of staff available to cover for lunch breaks.

Vegetable Products Committee

From October 1914 a nationwide campaign to provide fresh vegetables for soldiers, hospitals, and in particular sailors on warships, had been organised by the Vegetable Products Committee. The local receiving depot was the Swindon market and goods were left there by Thursday each week. It is not altogether surprising that it was a struggle to keep up the supply of produce from Swindon, which was neither a naval town nor a town with agricultural roots. By the end of May 1915, Swindon's contribution had fallen to 18 cwt in the month, which included a consignment of rhubarb from Daniel Kembrey and a consignment of onions from Mr Little in Wootton Bassett. A renewed campaign by the Swindon Vegetable Products Committee urged townsfolk to contribute to 'our gallant Jack Tars' by setting aside a small plot in their gardens. Representatives in the villages were encouraged to play their part. In October 1915 the Parish Council received a further request for fruit and vegetables. Mr Kembrey offered his premises as a free depot for receiving gifts, and he said that he would convey them to Swindon free of charge.

War Agricultural Committee

In Autumn 1915 the government called for all counties to establish War Agricultural Committees, as part of a nationwide initiative to maximise efficiency in food production. The Wiltshire County Committee periodically made requests of the Parish Council to meet its requirements, for example, in April 1916 they asked for assistance in supplying Scotch seed potatoes. Notices were duly placed in various parts of the town, and the Parish Council availed themselves of the Town Crier, but with no success. The Clerk complained that the information sent by the Committee was so inadequate that cooperation was impossible, and that the request had been made too late in the season for supply to be practical.

An Eyewitness Account from Germany

The Reverend G Roberts, recently released from Hamburg, gave a lecture on April 12th 1915 entitled "What I witnessed in Germany." The lecture was held in the Congregational Chapel with Alfred Ricks Humphries in the chair. At the end of the lecture, which was well attended and greatly appreciated by the audience, a hearty vote of thanks was proposed, and a collection was made in aid of the British and Foreign Sailors' Society.

The Story of 'George Hunt'

John Hartman Morgan of Priory Cottage, 28 Wood Street, vividly retells the story of a Wiltshireman who he met in the surgical tents of No 6 General at the No 19 Infantry Base Depôt in Rouen. Extracts from this story were published in the December 1915 edition of 'Nineteenth Century'. The full story was later published in 1916 in a chapter entitled 'The Wiltshires' in John's wonderful book 'Leaves from a Field Note-Book'. John tells us that:

The investiture of fiction has been here adopted; although the characters are 'real' (I can only hope that they will be half as real to the reader as they were and are to me) the names are assumed.

It is not coincidental that he chose the name George Hunt for his protagonist. It was, without doubt, the most common name in Wootton Bassett and the surrounding area. The other names which appear in this story, Scaplehorn and Twine, are both prevalent in the Wootton Bassett area. The parish adjacent to Wootton Bassett could be Brinkworth or Broad Town. Brinkworth is more likely because of the mention of Folly Wood. Medical records have not survived for the No 6 General hospital, so there is no evidence to be had there. The anonymity of the subject persists today, and all my attempts to identify him have failed, so I suspect that the story was fabricated, but based on real experiences. I include the story here in full, in the same spirit that it was originally told - to pay tribute to all those men who remain unknown.

"You talk to him, sir. He zeed a lot though he be kind o' mazed like now; he be mortal bad, I do think. But such a cheerful chap he be. I mind he used to say to us in the trenches: 'It bain't no use grousing. What mun be, mun be.' Terrible strong he were, too. One of our officers wur hit in front of the parapet, and we coulden get 'n in nohow - 'twere too hot; and Hunt, he unrolled his puttees and made a girt rope of 'em and threw 'em over the parapet and draw'd en in. Ah! that a did."

It was in one of the surgical tents of "No. 6 General" at the base. The middle of the ward was illuminated by an oil-lamp, shaped like an hour-glass, which shed a circle of yellow radiance upon the faces of the nurse and the orderly officer, as they stood examining a case-sheet by the light of its rays. Beyond the penumbra were rows of white beds, and in the farthest corner lay the subject of our discourse. "Can I talk to him?" I said to the nurse. "Yes, if you don't stay too long," she replied briskly, "and don't question him too much. He's in a bad way; his wounds are very septic."

He nodded to me as I approached. At the head of the bed hung a case-sheet and temperature-chart, and I saw at a glance the superscription-

Hunt, George, Private, No. 1578936 B Co. ...... Wiltshires.

I noticed that the temperature-line ran sharply upwards on the chart.

"So you're a Wiltshireman?" I said. "So am I." And I held out my hand. He drew his own from beneath the bedclothes and held mine in an iron grip.

"What might be your parts, sir?"

"W..... B....."

His eyes lighted up with pleasure. "Why, zur, it be nex' parish; I come from B...... I be main pleased to zee ye, zur."

"The pleasure is mine," I said. "When did you join?"

"I jined in July last year, zur. I be a resarvist."

"You have been out a long time, then?"

"Yes, though it do seem but yesterday, and I han't seen B..... since. I mind how parson, 'e came to me and axed, 'What! bist gwine to fight for King and Country, Jarge?' And I zed, 'Yes, sur, that I be - for King and Country and ould Wiltshire. I guess we Wiltshiremen be worth two Gloster men any day though they do call us 'Moon-rakers.' Not but what the Glosters ain't very good fellers," he added indulgently. "Parson, he be mortal good to I; 'e gied I his blessing and 'e write and give I all the news of the parish. He warnt much of a preacher though a did say 'Dearly beloved' in church in a very taking way as though he were a-courting."

"What was I a-doin', zur? Oh, I wur with Varmer Twine, head labr'er I was. Strong? Oh yes, zur, pretty fair. I mind I could throw a zack o' vlour ower my shoulder when I wur a boy o' vourteen. Why! I wur stronger then than I be now. 'Twas India that done me."

"Is it a large farm?" I asked, seeking to beguile him with homely thoughts.

"Six 'undred yackers. Oh yes, I'd plenty to do, and I could turn me hands to most things, though I do say it. There weren't a man in the parish as could beat I at mowing or putting a hackle on a rick, though I do say it. And I could drive a straight furrow too. Heavy work it were. The soil be stiff clay, as ye knows, zur. This Vlemish clay be very loike it. Lord, what a mint o' diggin' we 'ave done in they trenches to be sure. And bullets vlying like wopses zumtimes."

"Are your parents alive?" I asked.

"No, zur, they be both gone to Kingdom come. Poor old feyther," he said after a pause. "I mind 'un now in his white smock all plaited in vront and mother in her cotton bonnet—you never zee 'em in Wiltshire now. They brought us all up on nine shillin' a week - ten on us we was."

"I suppose you sometimes wish you were back in Wiltshire now?" I said.

"Zumtimes, sir," he said wistfully. "It'll be about over with lambing season, now," he added reflectively. "Many's the tiddling lamb I've a-brought up wi' my own hands. Aye, and the may'll soon be out in blossom. And the childern makin' daisy-chains."

"Yes," I said. "And think of the woods - the bluebells and anemones! You remember Folly Wood?"[11]

He smiled. "Ah, that I do: I mind digging out an old vixen up there, when 'er 'ad gone to earth, and the 'ounds with their tails up a-hollering like music. The Badminton was out that day. I were allus very fond o' thuck wood. My brother be squire's keeper there. Many a toime we childern went moochin' in thuck wood - nutting and bird-nesting. Though I never did hold wi' taking more'n one egg out of a nest, and I allus did

---

[11] Folly Wood is on the Brinkworth road, not far at all from Wootton Bassett, and this suggests that 'Varmer Twine' could be Frederick Charles Twine who is known to have owned Folly Wood in 1921.

*wet my vinger avore I touched the moss on a wren's nest. They do say as
the little bird 'ull never go back if ye doant."*

*His mind went roaming among childhood's memories and his eyes took
on a dreaming look.*

*"Mother, she were a good woman - no better woman in the parish, parson
did say. She taught us to say every night, 'Our Father, which art in
heaven' - I often used to think on it at night in the trenches. Them nights
- they do make you think a lot. It be mortal queer up there - you veels as
if you were on the edge of the world. I used to look up at the sky and
mind me o' them words in the Bible, 'When I conzider the heavens, the
work o' Thy vingers and the stars which Thou hast made, what is man
that Thou art mindful of him?' One do feel oncommon small in them
trenches at night."*

"I suppose you've had a hot time up there?"

"Ah that I have. And I zeed some bad things.""

"Bad?"

*"Cruel, sir, mortal cruel, I be maning. 'Twur dree weeks come Monday.
We wur in an advance near Wypers - 'bout as far as 'tis from our village
to Wootton Bassett. My platoon had to take a house. We knowed
'twould be hot work, and Jacob Scaplehorn and I did shake hands.
'Jarge,' 'e zed, 'if I be took write to my wife and tell 'er it be the Lard's
will and she be not to grieve.' And I zed, 'So be, Jacob, and you'll do the
same for I.' Our Officer, Capt'n S..... T....., d'you know 'en, sir? No?
'E com from Devizes way, he wur a grand man, never thinking of hisself
but only of us humble chaps - he said, 'Now for it, lads,' and we
advances in 'stended order. We wur several yards apart, just loike we was
when a section of us recruits wur put through platoon drill, when I fust
jined the Army an' sergeant made us drill with skipping-ropes a-stretched*

out so as to get the spaces. And there wur a machine-gun in that there house - you know how they sputters. It cut down us poor chaps loike a reaper. Jacob Scaplehorn wur nex' me and I 'eerd 'un say 'O Christ Jesus' as 'e went over like a rabbit and 'e never said no more. 'E wur a good man, wur Scaplehorn" - he added musingly - "and 'e did good things. And some chaps wur down and dragging their legs as if they did'n b'long to 'em. I sort o' saw all that wi'out seeing it, in a manner o' spaking; 'twere only arterwards it did come back to me. There warn't no time to think. And by the toime we got to thic house there were only 'bout vifteen on us left. We had to scrouge our way in through the buttry winder and we 'eerd a girt caddle inside, sort o' scuffling; 'twere the Germans makin' for the cellar. And our Capt'n posted some on us at top of cellar steps and led the rest on us up the stairs to a kind o' tallet where thuck machine-gun was. And what d'ye think we found, sir?" he said, raising himself on his elbow.

"What?"

"There was a poor girl there - half daft she wur - wi' nothing on but a man's overcoat. And she rushed out avore us on the landing and began hammering with her hands against a bedroom door and it wur locked. We smashed 'en in wi' our rifle-butts, and God's mercy! we found a poor woman there, her mother seemingly, with her breast all bloody an' her clothes torn. I could'n mak' out what 'er wur saying but Capt'n 'e told us as the Germans 'ad ravished her. We used our field-dressings and tried to make the poor soul comfortable and Capt'n 'e sent a volunteer back for stretcher-bearers."

"And what about the Germans?" I asked.

"Ah, I be coming to that, zur. Capt'n says, 'Now, men, we're going to reckon with those devils down below.' And we went downstairs and he stood at top of cellar-steps, 'twere mortal dark, an' says, 'Come on up out

o' that there.' And they never answered a word, but we could 'ear 'em breathing hard. We did'n know how many there were and the cellar steps were main narrow, as narrow as th' opening in that tent over there. So Capt'n 'e says, 'Fetch me some straw, Hunt.' 'Twere a kind o' farmhouse and I went out into the backside and vetched some. And Capt'n and us put a lot of it at top of steps and pushed a lot more vurther down, using our rifles like pitchforks and then 'e blew on his tinder and set it alight. 'Stand back, men,' he says, 'and be ready for 'em with the bay'net.' 'Tweren't no manner o' use shooting; 'twere too close in there and our bullets might ha' ricochayed. We soon 'eerd 'em a-coughing. There wur a terrible deal o' smoke, and there wur we a-waiting at top of them stairs for 'em to come up like rats out of a hole. And two on 'em made a rush for it and we caught 'em just like's we was terriers by an oat-rick; we had to be main quick. 'Twere like pitching hay. And then three more, and then more. And none on us uttered a word.

"An' when it wur done and we had claned our bay'nets in the straw, Capt'n 'e said, 'Men, you ha' done your work as you ought to ha' done.'"

He paused for a moment. "They be bad fellows," he mused. "O Christ! they be rotten bad. Twoads they be! I never reckon no good 'ull come to men what abuses wimmen and childern. But I'm afeard they be nation strong - there be so many on 'em."

His tale had the simplicity of an epic. But the telling of it had been too much for him. Beads of perspiration glistened on his brow. I felt it was time for me to go. I sought first to draw his mind away from the contemplation of these tragic things.

"Are you married?" I asked. The eyes brightened in the flushed face. "Yes, that I be, and I 'ave a little boy, he be a sprack little chap."

"And what are you going to make of him?"

"I'm gwine to bring un up to be a soldjer," he said solemnly. "To fight them Germans," he added. He saw the great War in an endless perspective of time; for him it had no end. "You will soon be home in Wiltshire again," I said encouragingly. He mused. "Reckon the Sweet Williams 'ull be out in the garden now; they do smell oncommon sweet. And mother-o'-thousands on the wall. Oh-h-h." A spasm of pain contracted his face. The nurse was hovering near and I saw my time was up. "My dear fellow," I said lamely, "I fear you are in great pain."

"Ah!" he said, "but it wur worth it."

The next day I called to have news of him. The bed was empty. He was dead.

Summer Fun and Fetes

The first weeks of August 1915 were rainy and miserable, and many thoughts must have turned to the anniversary of the war, but as the summer holidays began, town life continued much as it always had. On August 4th, the first anniversary of the war, the monthly market, held by Auctioneers Messrs Teagle and Sons in the High Street, offered a record number of cattle. There was a large attendance of farmers and cattle dealers. 70 of the 75 cattle in the ring were sold successfully. An entry of particular note was a group of 29 cattle offered by Hervey William White of Bynoll Farm, who was reducing the animals in his overstocked fields. On the same day, the children of the Church Schools were enjoying their annual treat in the Vicarage grounds in Station Road. Rain fell for a few minutes, then the skies cleared for the rest of the afternoon. The children had a picnic, played games, competed in races and had a very happy time. On the 5th August the church choir, accompanied by the Reverend Mathias and Mr Marchant, held their annual outing. They went by brake to Avebury, where they were welcomed by Mr C Bartlett from Broad

Hinton, and were given a luncheon and tea in a spacious barn lent by Mr Parsons. They visited Silbury Hill, and the Druid remains, then enjoyed a very pleasant drive back to Wootton Bassett. The children of the Wesleyan Sunday School also had their summer treat on the 5th of August, but due to the inclement weather, it was held in the schoolroom.

A few weeks later, the miserable weather and dramatic storms had passed. The Deanery enjoyed perfect summer weather for their garden party and sale of work in the Vicarage grounds on Thursday afternoon August 19 1915, to raise funds for the Church Missionary Society Medical Missions. The garden party was organised by Emilie Mathias, the vicar's daughter. It attracted about 300 visitors, mainly ladies from the surrounding area. Mrs Raines from Bowood opened the sale, giving a speech in which she told the ladies that her two sons were serving in the forces, one in the trenches in France, and the other in the Royal Flying Corps. She acknowledged that most of the guests were donating money to help the Belgians or send comforts to the soldiers and sailors, but they ought not to forget their other charitable duties. The teas were organised by Mrs Little and Miss Armstrong with help 'cutting up' from Mrs Bailey. There were a range of needlework, provisions, and other stalls, run by local ladies and church groups from Bradenstoke, Yatesbury, and Lyneham. The event raised a magnificent sum of over £55. The proceeds of the tea and gate money alone amounted to over £6. The work stall raised over £8.14s.3d. A patriotic stall which included articles made from a Canadian soldier's uniform by Florence Tayler of Bank House raised £2.7s.7d. Flower and fruit stalls raised over £1.7s.10d. A sweet stall raised 11s.3d. A literature stall selling Church Missionary Society books raised over 9s. The Young People's Union stall sold lavender and other scents for soldiers raising 13s.1d, and they exhibited a model Chinese Street and Japanese Village, raising a further 2s.7d. Yet more proceeds were raised through competitions, lemonade sales, an entertainment entitled 'Changing China', including a young ladies' Bible Class choir, and a collection. Canon McMillan later proposed a vote of thanks to the organisers and helpers. He said that this was the second year of the greatest war the world had ever seen and that he was certain that the lady stallholders had already been engaged in work for the war. He proposed that the work they were doing that afternoon was even more important than war work since missionary work was crucial for the prevention of future scourges of mankind such as this war. They had done something that day to send the Gospel to some who knew not the truth.

Fundraising, Flags, and Roses

Flag days were a very popular means of raising funds and were often dedicated to a nation in distress. Mrs Easley and a team of ladies eagerly undertook a sale of flags to raise funds for the Serbian Relief Fund in July 1915. The fund was to alleviate civilian suffering, and much of the money raised was to be sent to hospitals in Serbia. Considering the many calls on public generosity at that time, the ladies did remarkably well, raising £8 11s. The money was forwarded to the Mayor of Swindon, who sent back a sincere letter of thanks. On a Saturday in October 1915, the ladies of the town were again busy selling flags, this time in aid of the French Fund. The organiser was Mrs Florence Tayler, and the collectors included Miss Emilie Mathias and her dog Gyp.

A collection was made in the town for blind sailors and soldiers in July 1916. This was organised by Mrs Easley with a team of energetic workers. In spite of the inclement weather, the collection raised a magnificent sum, over £13.

Alexandra Rose Day was a charitable event instituted by Queen Alexandra in 1912 to mark the 50th anniversary of her arrival from

Denmark. Artificial wild roses made by the disabled were sold to raise money for the London hospitals, Queen Alexandra's favourite cause. The event gained greater importance during the war and was enthusiastically supported in Wootton Bassett. For the fifth Alexandra Rose Day on Saturday 10th June 1916, the sale of roses in Wootton Bassett was organised by Lucy Humphries. It was a great success, raising just over £14.7s, which included 18s.9d raised by selling wreaths for the hats of the rose sellers. A letter of thanks was written by Mr W Butt, secretary of the Swindon Hospital Aid Committee:

On behalf of the above committee, I am thanking you for the splendid effort you have made in organising Rose Day in Wootton Bassett; also your ladies who helped you to get such a magnificent total, which I am pleased to inform you is on top of the districts.

The Rose Day collection in aid of Swindon Victoria Hospital was repeated in 1917 under the direction of Mrs Easley, as Lucy Humphries was indisposed, and raised a similar amount: £13 10s 8½d.

War Savings

The War Savings Committee was a parliamentary initiative to encourage the British public to lend money to the government in support of the war effort. A meeting was held in Wootton Bassett on August 9th 1915 with a view to encouraging subscriptions and establishing a local committee. The large audience was greatly interested in the speeches delivered by Mr W Browning and Mr W T Tongbee. In November 1916 a well attended War Savings meeting was held at the Town Hall to discuss the forming of an Area Committee and the creation of a number of war savings associations in the town and its neighbouring villages, in line with the rest of the county. The County War Savings Committee presented the arguments in favour of the scheme. Reverend Hewlett Cooper, the rector of Tockenham, was particularly encouraging, speaking of the country's urgent need for funds. His passion may have been a factor in the subsequent invitation issued to him to become the organising secretary for the new Area Committee. He agreed to do so on a temporary basis until a permanent committee had been formed. The Wootton Bassett War Savings Association was officially launched on 6th February 1917. Its offices, care of George James Watts at 22 High Street, were to open weekly on Tuesdays, between 5pm and 7pm. The secretary was Florence Tayler of the Bank House, with George's daughter Dorothy as her assistant. William Gough was appointed treasurer, and Harold Dale was appointed the chairman. The War Savings movement continued its good work in the town throughout the War.

Harvest Festival 1915

The Harvest service in the Parish Church on the Sunday evening of October 10th 1915 was a particularly moving occasion. The church had been beautifully decorated by ladies of the congregation. There was a large congregation who sang the hymns most heartily. The choir sang the 'Magnificat and Nunc Dimittis in D' written by the brother of the church's organist William Timbrell Baxter, composer Frederick Nathaniel Baxter from Tetbury. The Reverend C A Mayall, the vicar of Swindon, preached a sermon, which included the following words:

This has been a year of sadness, for thousands and thousands of our young men have been called away to their long home. They came forward to conquer or to die, and it is through the kindness of Almighty God and the sacrifice of those young men that we have been allowed to gather in the blessings of the harvest. But we have had our agonising tidings, the tidings that someone has laid down his life for his country. Throughout the time of these troubles, God has been watching over us and providing for our needs. We know that 'all things work together for good to them that love God', but sometimes the way is dark, and we can not understand this,

*and we can not understand that. But let us wait till the final curtain
falls, then we shall understand that all things have been, "working for the
good for them that love God." We are reaping today what our forefathers
sowed. Someone must do the sowing; we can not always be reaping. The
flowers which a man sows are not gathered by his own hand. Those
soldiers are sowing the seed today in France and the Dardanelles so that
the generations of those that come after should reap the harvest.*

The collections, amounting to £4.11s.6d, were forwarded to the
Victoria Hospital, Swindon, and on Monday morning the gifts of jam,
butter, honey, eggs, cake, bread, tea, vegetables, and fruit were
conveyed to the Victoria Hospital by Mr James Tayler.

The War Years - 1916

Conscription and the Tribunals

Thus far through the war, service had been voluntary. Men were encouraged to volunteer and enlist in the Services. The Military Service Act changed all that by introducing compulsory enlistment, known as conscription. From January 1916 single men aged 18 to 41 years old were compelled to attest unless they were widowed with children, or ministers of religion. Some of these men were posted immediately; others were allowed to remain in civilian life on the Reserve, until such time as they might be called upon for duty. Any men who believed they had appropriate justification for exemption were required to register with their local tribunal before March 2nd 1916. The permitted grounds included performing civilian work of national importance, domestic hardship, health, and conscientious objection. In June 1916 conscription was extended to include married men.

The town held its own local tribunals to adjudicate claims for exemption. These were hosted by the Cricklade and Wootton Bassett Rural Tribunal during their Friday sessions at the Police Court in Station Road. After the war, the tribunal's records were destroyed in accordance with Government instructions, but thankfully many accounts of the cases it adjudicated are recorded, sometimes verbatim, in the pages of the local newspapers.

The chairman of the tribunals was usually Vice Admiral William Wilson. He was born in Over Worton, Oxfordshire, in 1848, and remained Lord of Over Worton until 1911. He married Frances Agnes Goddard in 1874, and through her came to live at the Manor House in Clyffe Pypard. He was a Naval Lieutenant for fifteen years and a Commander for nearly eight years. He headed the first recruitment meeting in Wootton Bassett and was the Chairman of the town's

Police Court. He was a Justice of the Peace the Guardian and Rural District Councillor for Clyffe Pypard until 1917 when he resigned due to his age. Reports of the day suggest that he was a wise, firm and just man, but his dry sense of humour is evident in the tribunal reports. Some of his delightful comments include: "You would look very nice in khaki. You fully consider that." One young cowman admitted that as it happened, he would not mind joining up. "Then you go, my son," replied Admiral Wilson, "and I hope you will kill many Germans." He must have commanded a great deal of respect throughout the area. Admiral Wilson died at the Manor House on 21st July 1921.[12]

Details of some 50 cases at the first tribunal were reported in the Herald on March 17th 1916. Regrettably, the early reports do not give the names of the men, but the vast majority were local farmers. Admiral Wilson was the Chairman, and the other members present were Mr C Bunce, Mr A Dunsford, Mr A T Giles, Mr E A Lucas, Mr E Pritchard and Daniel Kembrey, with the Clerk Robert Collins Hawkes. The military authorities were represented by Mr M J Crewe-Wood of Swindon. Other officers who served in the Wootton Bassett tribunal later in 1916 were Henry John Horton from Costow Farm, and Mr S Freegard, who represented the agricultural interests. At the

---

12 Admiral Wilson's son and heir William Werden Wilson, was born on the 7th of January 1887 in Dartmouth. He commenced his training as a Naval Cadet on HMS Britannia at the age of 14 and went on to serve in the Royal Navy. In July 1914 he was Commander of the 10,850 ton Argyll cruiser in the Third Cruiser Squadron. By November 1914 he was Commander of the 590 ton torpedo destroyer Garry where he remained until June 1915. He then became Commander of the larger 935 ton torpedo destroyer Owl. He was mentioned in the Naval Honour Sheets for his service on the Owl, escorting the Portuguese Expeditionary Force to France 'in a very satisfactory manner'. For this action he was Gazetted on the 4th of February 1921 (CW/1349). William's first wife was Sophie Irene Whittemore, by whom he had four children. William remarried to Rose Margaret Masterman in 1936. William inherited the Manor on the death of his mother Frances in 1940. On his death in 1950 the Manor passed on to his son Peter. He is buried at Clyffe Pypard.

Wiltshire Appeal Tribunal, Captain F G Morley represented the National Service Department.

Local recruitment officers increasingly looked towards Wiltshire's fit and healthy young farmers for a supply of new soldiers. Systems were evolved to provide substitute workers in order to free up those farmers who were eligible to serve. The substitution officer worked in co-operation with a local agricultural committee, generally including at least one experienced farmer, to supply a suitable worker. The substitution officer was not a military representative, nor was he an agricultural expert. He relied upon the agricultural committee for advice and local knowledge. In general, recruitment officers were not supposed to call up a farmer until a substitute had actually arrived on the farm and begun work. Employers had the right to give any substitute a trial before hiring him, and wages were fixed before the engagement was completed. Inevitably the process was hampered by a dearth of suitable substitutes, and tribunals were forced to work creatively within the rules to the circumstances. At critical times, such as harvest, farmers could apply for a soldier to be released from service to help out.

A Volunteer Training Corps Route March

About fifty members of the Swindon B Company of the Volunteer Training Corps came to Wootton Bassett on a route march on a Wednesday afternoon in February 1916. They were met by the local members, led by Quarter-Master-Sergeant Underhill, together with representatives from around the area including Mr C Bartlett from Broad Hinton and Private Hunt from Lyneham. The party enjoyed a substantial tea at the Red Lion Assembly Rooms, followed by a very enjoyable musical evening, including songs by Mr Bartlett, Mr Bickham, Mr Wiltshire, Mr Price, and others. Scout Thomas Fricker from 65 High Street was greatly applauded for his rendition of "When

I Come Back", with the boy Scouts joining in with the chorus. After a thoroughly pleasant evening, the volunteers returned to Swindon by train.

War Work for Women

As the war progressed, it became increasingly difficult for employers to find suitable staff. Many local businesses found that their workforce had dwindled to a handful of old men and a few young lads. Many women must have been keen to take up employment, and the war opened doors to opportunities which had previously been denied to them. Several took charge of their husband's businesses in their absence. I have found, for example, references to women running their husband's shop, or taking over their husband's pub, some becoming licensees in their own right. Some found new employment locally; others travelled into Swindon to work in the munitions factory and other businesses. The local Councils played a role in regulating and encouraging the employment of women. At a meeting of the Rural District Council in November 1915, a letter was read by the Rural District Councils Association urging employers to give preference to the relatives of those who had enlisted when taking on women in clerical and commercial work to replace men who had joined up. The Parish Council placed a notice in the window of the Clerk's Office in January 1916 inviting female volunteers to assist with farm work and war food societies.

There was a feeling that the gravity of the present situation, and the possible developments of the future, made it incumbent on all to view these proposals with sympathy, and to render the most vigorous aid possible, and the Council will be grateful if some patriotic woman will come forward, ready herself to engage in farm work and encourage others in the same direction, and generally to assist in making use of the means and instructions for accomplishing these ends offered by certain public authorities or by the patriotism of private individuals.

Lighting Restrictions

For a year now lighting regulations were in place, under the Defence of the Realm Regulations, known as DORA, introduced in 1915. The regulations applied to districts all around the country, particularly in coastal areas, where there were genuine fears of Zeppelin strikes and naval attacks. The specific details were left to regional authorities to decide. Some authorities were stricter than others, and there was occasionally unrest and dissent, particularly when traders felt they were being targeted and that trade was being adversely affected. In 1916 new local lighting regulations were imposed in Wootton Bassett. The changes were not particularly onerous but necessitated some minor compromises, for example, the vicar and churchwardens decided to move the Sunday evening service to 3pm, and the weekly intercession service on Thursdays was moved to 4.15pm. Similarly, the Free Churches moved their Sunday evening service to 5.45pm.

The regulations not only required the shading or extinguishing of lights emanating from property but also banned the use of 'powerful' lights on vehicles. New requirements were to show illuminated lamps on all vehicles, including red rear lamps on bicycles. The first local prosecution under the Regulations took place in May 1916, and the defendant was Annie Gibbs of Church Street. Annie was summoned for riding a bike without a rear light on April 20th. Superintendent Millard was at pains to point out that the proceedings were not taken under the ordinary Lights on Vehicles Act but under the Defence of the Realm Regulations, which had been in force three or four months. They had given everyone a chance, he said. Police Constable Culley's evidence stated that he had seen the defendant in the High Street.

When he first called to her to stop, she had taken no notice, but when he shouted again, she stopped. Annie was fined 1 shilling.

Lighting restrictions continued throughout the war. Wootton Bassett's tradesmen decided that from September 30th 1918 they would close their establishments early during the winter months, due to the ongoing lighting restrictions. Until the end of March 1919, they closed at 6pm on Mondays, Tuesdays and Wednesdays, and at 8pm on Fridays and Saturdays.

Lord Kitchener's death

The shocking news of Lord Kitchener's tragic death on Monday the 5th June 1916 reached Wootton Bassett on the following afternoon. Kitchener, who was Secretary of State for War, was killed when HMS Hampshire, the ship which was taking him to diplomatic negotiations in Russia, was sunk near the Orkney Islands, by a mine laid by a German U-boat. In the evening, a rumour spread that he had been saved, but unhappily this hope was short-lived. The flag on St Bartholomew's Church was dropped to half-mast as a mark of the town's grief and respect. At the Church the following Sunday the Reverend Mathias referred to Lord Kitchener's death with feeling at both the morning and evening services. He said:

In common with the whole Empire, we as a congregation would like to show our loving respect to the memory of the great man who so nobly answered the call of the nation at perhaps the most critical moment of its existence. Lord Kitchener did wonderful work; the raising of 5,041,000 volunteers was beyond all expectations. The lead he gave in self-sacrifice by taking the war pledge to abstain from all alcoholic liquors was most praiseworthy. The risks he continually ran in crossing the Channel were very great, and ended in the fatal venture to consolidate the interests of the Allies.

At the conclusion of each service, the organist, William Timbrell Baxter, played Handel's Dead March from Saul.

Christmas 1916

Christmas fat cattle markets were a seasonal event in North Wiltshire. Wootton Bassett's 1916 market was rather an impressive one, despite the war. The Herald describes it in detail:

As usual, the market was held in the wide street of the old town, and for two hours, the scene was a very busy one. Farmers were present from all over the countryside, and with them were dealers and a good sprinkling from the adjacent towns. The Cabinet crisis had left the farmers unmoved, and the chief subject in their minds was business, especially the prices of cattle and the increasing costs of feeding stuffs. All the livestock was sold by auction, and clearances were effected. So far as the quality and number of stock were concerned, the market was the best for some years. Pigs were more numerous than usual, but only a few good bacon pigs were on sale. The supply of calves was fairly good.

Owing to the lighting restrictions there was no meat show this year, but the butchers laid in some good supplies of meat and poultry for Christmas. Mrs W Drury, High Street, is showing two prime fat heifers from Swindon Christmas market, two heifers fed by Mr Henry Gaisford (Tockenham), one fed by Mr Hosier (Tockenham), and two from Calne Christmas market, together with 10 fat tegs (two-year-old sheep) bought at Malmesbury Christmas market. There is also a large stock of fat turkeys, geese and chickens. Mr G A Angelinetta, High Street, has two prime maiden heifers from Calne Christmas market, and one from Tetbury Christmas market, and also a number of sheep from Tetbury, with a fine lot of turkeys, ducks, geese, fowls, rabbits etc.

On Christmas morning the Bread Charity made its usual distribution to all persons in receipt of Parish Relief in the Parish Office. On

December 28th the Trustees of the Poor Stock Charity, namely Reverend Mathias, Daniel Kembrey, and Mr T Bartlett, distributed about £33 to the second poor at the Town Hall.

The tradition of the Christmas Dinner Table Collection is one which is unfamiliar today but has a great deal to recommend it. Edith Pye of 150 High Street and Kate Little of 37 High Street held a collection in aid of Lord Roberts' Memorial Workshops Extension Fund. The fund was established after the Boer War to help disabled soldiers and sailors to earn a living through self-supporting workshops. It was now under pressure to raise additional funds to cope with the influx of disabled servicemen. The Table Collection raised £8.

The War Years - 1917

A Memorial Service

A combined memorial service for all the congregations of the town was held at the Parish Church at 7.30pm on Wednesday, 7th February 1917. The Vicar invited the people to submit the names of casualties they would like to be remembered. By the time an announcement was published in the Parish Magazine, 20 names had already been submitted.

A large number of people of all denominations attended the service despite the severe wintry weather. There were united choirs, and the Reverend E Parsons (Primitive Methodist) and the Rev J Perry (Congregationalist) assisted Reverend Mathias by reading the lessons. The impressive service began with the hymn 'Let Saints on Earth', after which the opening sentences of the burial service were read and Psalms 33 and 146 were sung. Then came the first lesson by the Rev J Perry, the hymn 'On the Resurrection Morning', the second lesson by the Rev E Parsons, and the hymn 'Now the Labourer's Task is O'er'.

Next followed an address by Reverend Mathias. He took for his text, 'Greater love hath no man than this, that a man lay down his life for his friends'. He said the object of the service was first to show their respect and gratitude to those who had died for them, and also to show sympathy with those who had lost their loved ones. What did these departed heroes expect from us? First, sympathy and gratitude, as manifested by this service; secondly, they expected us to exact such a peace as would ensure that they had not made their great sacrifice in vain, and also that our Government would provide for their families, their aged parents, and all those depending on them. In conclusion, the Vicar said this war was teaching us to lead less selfish lives. Life was a nobler thing and money a better thing when spent for others.

The following list of heroes was then read: Oliver Ernest Angelinetta, Gilbert Angelinetta, Charles Barnes, Christopher Blanchett, W E Burchell, Hedley Brown, Godfrey Arthur Ephraim William Bridgeman, Ernest Sidney Cox, Henry Gibbs, Harry Hunt, Clarence Hunt, Reginald Hunt, Archibald Harry Hunt, Edward Helps (sic), Charles Henry Hughes, John Hird, Albert Hewer, George Edward Lovelock, Charles Lovelock, Jesse Lawrence, Albert Peaple, Rupert Charles Rowe, George Sawyer, Arthur Sidney Twine, William Howard Twine, and Edgar James Wright. The service concluded with the sentences and prayers of the burial service, and the organist, William Timbrell Baxter, played the Dead March in Saul. The Parish Magazine recorded that from comments made, the service appeared to have been a very acceptable token of 'Parochial Sympathy and respect for our fallen heroes and their families'.

Recruitment

At the Parish Meeting on Wednesday, 28th March 1917, there was a lively discussion about the proposal to canvass the town in favour of national service. Much of the talk was about the errors which had been made in 'putting men in the wrong places'. It was largely agreed that there were few in the parish who were not already engaged in some sort of national service, so when Richard Parsons proposed, and Mr M Watts seconded that the parish should do its best to promote voluntary enrolment, and that the Parish Council should be asked to make the required canvass, the vote unsurprisingly went against the proposal by eight votes to six.

Queen Mary's Army Auxiliary Corps

The Women's Army Auxiliary Corps was formed in February 1917 and was renamed the Queen Mary's Army Auxiliary Corps on 9th April 1918. In total, 57,000 women joined the corps. I have only found one member locally, Annie Louisa Telling.[13] Members served mainly in Britain, but in 1917 fourteen women served as cooks and waitresses on the front in France, and in 1918 some women served on the front in medical roles. The Corps was disbanded on 27th September 1921.

The Women's Land Army

In April 1917 a national campaign to recruit women for National Service in the Women's Land Army was launched. The local newspapers ran advertisements proclaiming, '10,000 Women Wanted at Once to grow and Harvest the Victory Crops'. The requirement was for 5000 milkers, 4000 field workers and 1000 carters. Women who enrolled immediately would be given a free outfit, high boots, breeches, overall and a hat. They would receive maintenance during training and travel expenses in connection with their work. Wages of 18 shillings a week, or the district rate, whichever was higher, would be paid. The farms and their accommodation would be inspected and approved by the Women's County Committee of the Board of Agriculture. There were prospects for promotion and the promise of special facilities for settlement at home or overseas at the end of the War. The campaign was very successful, and it is quite likely that some local girls were recruited. In December 1917 a mass meeting was held in Devizes to celebrate the achievements of the scheme. About 250 women attended from all parts of the county. The Countess of Pembroke awarded badges and 29 girls who had been working on the land for over a year were awarded stripes by The Right Honourable Rowland Edmund Prothero MP, President of the Board of Agriculture. Mr Prothero gave an encouraging speech, in which he praised the girls, who were, 'among the wisest of their generation'. Whereas once farmers had been reluctant to take on women workers,

---

[13] For Annie Louisa Telling's story see Breach Lane in the Country companion volume.

all prejudices had now gone and farmers knew that women could 'stick it'. In December 1916, he said, agriculturally speaking, all was gloom depression and uncertainty. Their men were being taken from them, they did not know where they were, and there was every symptom that there would be a heavy decline in production. However, the farmers had rolled up their sleeves and worked hard to reverse the threat, producing more corn, wheat, barley, oats, roots, peas and potatoes than in 1916. He acknowledged the inestimable service that farmers had rendered to the nation and for the war.

The Food Economy Campaign

As food shortages became more acute around the country, talks and cookery demonstrations were held to encourage a pragmatic response from homes and businesses. In early June 1917, a representative assembly met in the Town Hall to discuss the Food Economy Campaign, with the prominent local grocer Edward Henry Radbone presiding. Mr Radbone drew attention to the serious situation in regard to the food supply and hoped all present would practice strict economy. It was unanimously decided that one of the best ways to co-operate in this matter would be to hold food saving demonstrations at a convenient centre in the town. A large and influential committee was set up to undertake this work including schoolmaster John Sanders Searle as Secretary, and Mr Richard Tom Tayler of Lloyds Bank as treasurer. Several subscriptions were promised at the Close of the meeting, and the committee advertised that they would be glad of further financial assistance from anyone interested in the campaign.

A cookery demonstration, the first in a series arranged by the Reverend Hewlett Cooper, was held in the Wesleyan School in Wootton Bassett on the Friday at the beginning of July 1917. The promoters were Mr E Radbone and Mr R Little. Reverend Hewlett Cooper introduced the meeting by setting forth some of the main features of the food economy campaign, illustrating his talk with an instructive series of diagrams and pictures. He explained the need to focus public attention on the grave situation and stated that amateur cooks should be encouraged to assist by collecting recipes and informing others about the use of food substitutes. Saving food was praiseworthy, but producing food from home resources was the more excellent way. He had been warning people of the national peril of under-cultivation of England's soil for ten years past. England was dependent on foreign supplies for 80% of its requirements, and we had been living in a regular fools' paradise. We must alter, or suffer, he concluded. Miss M G Breeze, who attended through the courtesy of the County Education Committee, then gave an excellent demonstration, speaking in a pleasing and instructive way on the proper preparation of different foods and their value in nourishing the body. She remarked that complaints about indigestion from maize and oatmeal would be unheard of if people masticated these nourishing foods more thoroughly. Next, there were illustrated explanations of the constituents and properties of different foods, and finally, the audience enjoyed looking at the stalls which had been set out. The demonstration was greatly appreciated, but somewhat less well attended than hoped for. The Herald commented bleakly,

No wonder at the lack of social effort and enthusiasm, no wonder at the drifting apart of employers and employed, when in such times as these, there is little public concern to shake off the blight of apathy which settles on the less conscientious inhabitants of some rural places.

The second demonstration took place a week later in the Wesleyan Schoolroom. Miss Breeze gave a practical demonstration on the topic of meat substitutes, which was watched by an appreciative assembly.

As grave food shortages increasingly threatened the county of Wiltshire, pressure mounted to get locals to produce their own food.

In November 1917 the parish clerk was instructed to send the County Agricultural Committee the names of owners of uncultivated gardens and allotments. In March 1918 Mr C H Corbett of the County Food Control Committee attended the Annual Parish Meeting and spoke about the efforts the County Committee were making to ensure that every possible patch of uncultivated land was brought under cultivation. It was proposed that the town should establish a Food Production Committee composed of members of the Parish Council and others.

Harvest Thanksgiving

The Harvest Thanksgiving day at the Parish Church on Sunday 7th October 1917, was the fourth since War began. The offerings of bread, butter, eggs, jam, rabbits, grapes, pears, plums, apples, potatoes, marrows, carrots, and cabbages, were half as much again as the previous year. Mrs Bevir, Mrs Mundy and Mrs Dale decorated the chancel, the vicar's daughter Emilie Mathias decorated the pulpit, Lucy Humphries decorated the font, and Miss MacFarlane and Miss Tuckey decorated the porch. There were four services that day: a morning service conducted by the Rev Mathias, a midday Holy Communion, a children's service in the afternoon and an evening service conducted by Reverend Goddard of Clyffe Pypard, which was attended by a large congregation. Reverend Goddard's sermon commenced with the rather sombre Revelations 6:8:

And I looked, and beheld a pale horse: and his name that sat on him was Death, and Hell followed with him. And power was given unto them over the fourth part of the earth, to kill with sword, and with hunger, and with death, and with the beasts of the earth.

Reverend Goddard said:

This year has been a most prosperous one in many ways. The previous winter was unusually severe, lasting well into the spring, but this was followed by two months of glorious weather. Everything seemed set for an excellent harvest, but the weather has changed again, bringing unsettled weather rain. In the Wootton Bassett area hay is still standing in the fields, and in many cases has been spoiled, nevertheless we have harvested large quantities of fruit, and in other ways, there is a good deal to be thankful for. Consider the dangers you have been saved from, temptations you have resisted, difficulties you have overcome and sins you have been forgiven. Consider what has happened in France, Belgium, Serbia and Poland. Do you realise what has happened to France during the conquest in the Northern part? Do you realise the conditions in France with every man of military age called up to join the Army, and the work practically all done by women? In France, they have not only suffered from high prices, like we have, but have lost everything. Even the land has been ruined and will take many years to recover. When you think of these things, you have much to be thankful for. This district has never in my lifetime been so prosperous as it is now. We are asked to help the Prisoners of War Fund and the Red Cross, which all are glad to do. We are also called upon to give to other charitable objects so that they should not suffer. We can all of us try not to forget our peace duties in our war work.

After the services, the produce was conveyed by James Tayler to the Victoria Hospital in Swindon.

An Eyewitness Account from France

In November 1917 Army Padre Reverend J H Gavin of Swindon, who had recently returned from two years in France, gave a lantern lecture at the Council Schools, with vocal solos provided by Miss Elsie Drew. The event drew a huge and enthusiastic crowd, many being turned away for lack of space. The lantern operator was Mr A E Collins of

Swindon. The chair was occupied by Dr Watson, who introduced the speaker, saying that we owed a debt not only to the Army but to our magnificent Navy too. The proceeds of the lecture were divided between the local Belgian Fund and the Young People's Guild. Mr Gavin described his experience as a chaplain in France whilst showing many interesting photographs of places visited, and men who had earned distinction in the war. Mr Gavin described some of the achievements of local heroes whom he had met. He said that we owed a great deal to the men in France, who were doing, daring, and suffering so much.

National Children's Home Entertainment

On Tuesday, 4th December 1917 a large crowd attended a musical entertainment and gymnastic display at the Council Schools put on by Farnborough Band and the Choir of the National Children's Home and Orphanage. The Chairman for the event was Mr W Rabbetts of Broad Hinton. The boys acquitted themselves admirably, and their skill in gymnastics was much admired. Sister Beatrice Cowle gave a very interesting account of the work of the Home. She explained that it was founded by Dr Stephenson in 1869, and was now one of the largest child-saving institutions in the land. Children were admitted from all over the country, without regard to creed, and solely on the ground of need.

Christmas 1917

As Wootton Bassett prepared for a fourth Christmas at war, the town slipped into the routine of collecting for parcels for soldiers, sailors and prisoners of war like a well-oiled machine. On Christmas Day the Boy Scouts, organised by Scoutmaster A B Hunt, distributed envelopes for an after-dinner collection in aid of the Blinded Soldiers and Sailors Fund. A very good amount was raised. The eight Scouts who gave up part of their Christmas Day for this valuable work were J Norris, B Curtis, B Lawrence, S Barnes, C Brust, R Norris, N Dixon, and W Thompson.

The War Years - 1918

Conscription

At the end of February 1918, the lower registration age dropped to include boys who had attained the age of 15 years since August 15th 1915. The boys would not necessarily be required to fight but could be called up if needed for the forces or for industrial work. The higher age limit was raised to 51 years, and the definition of work of national importance was tightened up. In May 1918 men aged 43 and 44 were called up. These men had attested voluntarily but had hitherto been allowed to remain in civilian life. They received an individual notice calling them for medical examination. If their services were needed, they would be required to report for duty on the 15th day after medical grading. Applications for exemption were required to be sent no more than seven days after medical classification.

An Exciting Flying Demonstration

On April 3rd 1918 an aeroplane landed in Lydiard Tregoze due to engine trouble and remained there until Friday. Having completed the necessary repairs, the Canadian pilot gave the locals the finest demonstration of flying skills ever witnessed in the district, to the great admiration of a large crowd.

The London Regiment

From time to time Wootton Bassett enjoyed a visit from troops stationed at Chiseldon Camp. In January 1918 a party of this kind, consisting of non-commissioned officers and men of the London Regiment gave a Khaki Concert at the Council Schools. A collection was made for the Local Belgian Fund.

German Prisoners of War

The nearest military POW Camp to Wootton Bassett for German prisoners was at the Chiseldon military camp at Draycot Foliat, run by Major Ostler. At the time there were 210 prisoners of war in this camp. In 1918 the National Farmers Union held a meeting at the Goddard Arms in Swindon, to discuss the War Office scheme for the employment of German prisoners on the land. The Chairman of the NFU, Mr J E Stevens, invited Major Ostler to present the scheme to the local farmers within a radius of three to five miles of the camp, encompassing the eastern borders of the Wootton Bassett area. Major Ostler said that the prisoners were expected to walk to work if within three miles, and transport would be arranged for greater distances. They would take their own food and cooking pots but would need access to hot water and a fire. All the hours and rates of pay were set by the Army. If demand for labour were to exceed supply, he would be able to request more. Captain Jervaise also explained that it might be possible to set up canvas camps in outlying districts. In the event, several such camps were set up in March 1918.

'List of Places of Internment' published by the Prisoner of War Information Bureau in 1919 confirms the existence of a handful of sites for Combatant Prisoners of War which were independent of the military camps. All of these camps came under the control of a larger PoW camp at Dorchester, Dorset, and were divided into subgroups under a local Commandant. An agricultural group with its HQ in Shepton Mallet included Shepton Mallet agricultural camp, Hallatrow, the Austrian POW camp at Wookey, and a camp originally under canvas but later at The Old Corn Stores in Binegar. Another group was managed in Devizes and included agricultural camps in Devizes, Chippenham and Wootton Bassett. There was also an Austrian POW camp at Frome which was independent of any local group, and Barney

Farm near Ramsbury. The prisoners in these camps were generally recruited from among the internees in larger camps, using a trade testing party to determine their aptitudes. Security was the responsibility of men of the Royal Defence Corps, and men from the camp generally walked to local farms under the watch of a single armed guard. Prisoners' duties covered the usual seasonal range of agricultural activities. They were given payment, averaging at about 1.5 pence per day, as well as superior food rations.

The Wootton Bassett camp opened in March 1918 under the command of Second Lieut A Low. The camp was in a 'substantial stone building' in the town, hired for the purpose, called the Corner House. This may have been a pseudonym for the Red Lion Inn, as no more likely property has been identified.[14] There were 34 military prisoners of war in the Wootton Bassett camp, and 38 more were billeted with farmers in outlying farms under the 'B' Scheme. A further ten formed a migratory gang. Doctor Watson was the camp physician. Vizefeldwebel Waldemar Hoepfner, 93 Res Inf Regt, was the German camp leader and interpreter. During November 1918 the Wootton Bassett camp was the subject of an inspection by Dr A de Sturler, from the staff of the Swiss Legation. Dr de Sturler toured and inspected a number of camps in the South West including Wootton Bassett. His report is held at the National Archives, and all relevant contents are included here. He reported the condition of the camps as 'all good'. In Wootton Bassett, the sleeping arrangements were typical of other camps, and the prisoners were allowed four blankets. Most of the camps contained a supply of books, games and musical instruments. Among the camps Dr de Sturler inspected, Wootton Bassett's accommodation was ranged first, alongside Fair View at Devizes, for

---

[14] For more about the Red Lion, 59 High Street, see the Town companion volume.

the quality of its housing. The sanitary arrangements were satisfactory, and there were no complaints with regard to food. Wootton Bassett was unaffected by influenza at the time of the inspection, and the health of the prisoners was very good. The work in Wootton Bassett was only agricultural, with no general labouring, and the prisoners worked eight to nine hours a day. No complaints were made with regard to work or pay. The staff reported that the prisoners were well behaved and gave little or no trouble.

The Camp must have closed by March 1919. On March 5th 1919, a market day, Messrs Armstrong and Son held an auction in The Close, opposite the Police Station, on instructions from the Wiltshire War Agricultural Executive Committee. The Herald reports that the items for sale were from the Prisoners of War Camp, although it was not confirmed in the Herald's article or Armstrong's advertisement whether the lots were exclusively from the Wootton Bassett camp. There were about 260 lots, including machinery and plant, lorries built by the Bristol Wagon Works Company, other wagons, drills, binders, ploughs, rollers, mowers, cultivators, a quantity of leather including harnesses and collars, and supplies such as binder twine. Many of the items had been recently purchased and had never been used. Mr Trotman Howes and several members of the County Executive attended to direct the proceedings. The sale attracted a large gathering from Wiltshire and beyond. The lots changed hands very quickly, and high prices were paid.

Absent Military Voters

The Representation of the People Act of February 1918 extended the right to vote in national parliamentary elections to men aged 21 and over, whether or not they owned property, and to women aged 30 and over who lived in the constituency, or occupied land or premises with a rateable value above £5, or whose husbands did. At the same time, it extended the right to vote in local government elections to include women aged over 21 on the same terms as men. The names in the local rolls were probably canvassed between about June 1918 and about September 1918. Unfortunately, the full absent voters' list for our area has not survived. However, the standard electoral roll for 1918 contains the code NM for serving naval and military men, with an italic letter 'a' to indicate that they were absent for the December 1918 election.

There were 189 men listed in Wootton Bassett town who were still away fighting for their country during the closing months of the war. In addition, 10 men were listed in Tockenham, 28 in Broad Town and 53 in Lydiard Tregoze. All the details from these 1918 roll have been entered into the relevant households in the Residents volumes.

Remembrance Day 1918

On 4th August a Remembrance Day to mark four years of war was observed simultaneously by every denomination in the town. At the Parish Church, the morning service sermon was given by Reverend Currie Vicar of Hounslow, and the evening service sermon was given by Reverend L G Cawker of Broad Town. At the Congregational Chapel, the service was taken by Percy Pennis. The Primitive Methodist service was conducted by the recently installed Army Chaplain Reverend Richard Cowie, and at the Wesleyan Chapel Reverend H C Bassett preached in the morning and Mr Baker in the evening.

RSPCA Collection

A collection was made on August 7th 1918 for the RSPCA sick and wounded horses fund. The sum of £17 17s 5d was raised. The collectors were Mrs Rich, Miss Curtis, Miss Griffiths, Miss D Drury, Lucy Humphries, Mrs Bond, and Mrs Stevens.

After the War

November 11th 1918 is the day we all know today as Armistice Day.
The Herald describes the day in Wootton Bassett:

> *On Monday morning a deathly stillness seemed to be over the town.
> Everyone was waiting to hear the verdict of the Kaiser and his colleagues,
> and when it became known that the armistice had been signed and that
> hostilities were to cease, flags were soon flying in all directions, and the
> greatest excitement prevailed. Shopkeepers soon sold out of their stocks of
> flags and red, white and blue ribbons. It was good to hear the old church
> bells ring out in a joyous peal after four years' silence, and Messrs W
> Baxter and S Lawrence are to be highly commended on their promptitude
> in getting together, with some difficulty, enough men to ring them.*

At 8pm a united thanksgiving service, conducted by Reverend Mathias,
was held in the parish church. There was a very large congregation.
The service commenced with the singing of the doxology, and then
came the National Anthem and prayers of thanksgiving. Psalm 29 was
chanted, and John Sanders Searle read the lesson. The Te Deum was
heartily sung and also the hymns, 'All people that on earth do dwell',
and 'O God, our help in ages past'. Some thanksgiving prayers were
read, followed by the General Thanksgiving, which was repeated by
the whole congregation. The service throughout was of a hearty
nature, and expressions of thanksgiving were evident on all sides.

A united Free Church thanksgiving service was held at the Primitive
Methodist Chapel two days later, for which the building was crowded.
Mr Dennis, a Congregational Minister, conducted the service. The
meeting opened with the singing of the doxology, and the Reverend T
Bates of Brinkworth gave the address. The service ended with a lusty
rendition of the National Anthem.

Reverend Mathias invited all the free churches to attend united services at the Parish Church on following Sunday. It was unanimously decided to close all the other churches and exhort people to attend the Parish Church en masse. These united services of thanksgiving were held at on Sunday, 17th November 1918 the Parish Church. Holy Communion was celebrated at 8am and 11am. The service in the morning was conducted by Reverend Mathias. He preached an impressive sermon based on Psalm 124:

> *If it had not been the Lord who was on our side, when men rose up against us; Then they had swallowed us up quick, when their wrath was kindled against us; Then the waters had overwhelmed us, the stream had gone over our soul. Blessed be the Lord, who hath not given us as a prey to their teeth.*

The Herald reported the sermon in detail. Reverend Mathias said:

> *I do not know what your thoughts are, or feelings, but very probably I should not make a mistake if I said you were thinking the same as myself. First of all, it is with outside feelings of gratitude to Almighty God for His mighty working on our behalf. We cannot realise the war has come to such a rapid ending. Why is it He has delivered us out of this conflict? It has come to us with such a shock that we are unable to realise it, but little by little, we shall enjoy the full blessings of peace. This is the first Sunday we have been able to enjoy for four years, and the time is flying on. How many times I have been asked: "When can we have the clock striking again?" What hours of madness have been spent during that time! Six months ago the Kaiser gave his terms, and if he had won what would we have done? While we thank God with all our hearts, we must also thank the generous noble-hearted men of our navy, army and airmen for all their courageous bravery, and those who have given their lives for our safety. While we thank those who fought, we must also*

thank those who during the last four years have worked untiringly on munitions. I feel I cannot thank God enough for all His goodness.

The day of thanksgiving culminated in an impressive united evening service, conducted by Reverend Mathias. The bells rang a merry peal before the service began and the altar was beautifully decorated with roses and palms by Mrs Nora Twine of the Manor House. The church was packed with a crowded and earnest congregation, and the parish church's own choir was augmented by members of the Free Church choirs. Members of the Parish Council attended the service en masse including Mr Herron the chairman, Walter Richard Armstrong the vice-chairman, Mr G Wallis, Francis Teagle, Mr F Rich, Frank Bartlett, Daniel Kembrey, A R Strange, Mr W Walker, Mr G Smith, and Robert Little the Clerk. John Sanders Searle read the first lesson. Reverend Richard Cowie read the second lesson and also preached an excellent sermon from Psalm 103: 'Praise the Lord O my soul, and all that is within me praise His Holy Name'. Reverend Cowie said:

War is over. Humanity is upon its knees thanking God, and we lift up our hearts to Almighty God. As we look back on the four years and three months of the past war, we are like in a dream. We must acknowledge that God has been with us, although we may not all believe that He is our God. We thank God for those men who have laid down their lives, and we may think of those last rites that have been performed in their hundreds and thousands. As we are emerging into the New Year may it be one of many blessings, and may God give us grace that when He gives us peace, it may be a righteous and lasting peace. The call comes to us to praise God. We so often ask the Lord to bless us, and here is our opportunity - that we should bless God. We are able to give something to Him in return. He expects us to enter into His sanctuary. May we love Him in return. He maketh all things work together for good. Let it be praise from the soul and not only from the lips. Let us thank Him for the many mercies we have received, and the many blessings. How the Unseen Hand has pushed back the enemy, and what a most marvellous deliverance we have had! Let us remember His many blessings. If we measure them by our desires, we shall be filled with wonder, love and praise. Whilst bloodshed and hostilities have ceased, let us not forget His blessings.

The service closed with the National Anthem. A total of £12.10s.3d was raised by collections during the day, and this was given to the King's Fund for Disabled Soldiers and Sailors.

Peace Celebrations

Six months after Armistice Day, with the Peace Treaty still to be signed, the Council began to debate the form of the town's forthcoming peace celebrations. Eventually, they concluded that the public should determine this for themselves. They resolved to hold a public meeting to that effect, which duly took place in the Council Schools on Thursday, 5th June 1919, with Daniel Kembrey as chairman. John Thomas Page proposed a celebratory tea for the children, and it was suggested that the older residents should be included. After much discussion, it was decided to include children under 14 years and older residents over 60 years. Mr W Boyce suggested that all residents should be invited to a fête. Mr Flewelling proposed a motion to establish a peace celebrations committee, which was seconded by James Frank Underhill. All the members of the Parish Council were elected, as well as Harold Dale, Mr W Boyce, Mr E Newman, Mr C Curtis, Mr M Sheppard, Howard Horsell, Mr A Curtis, Mr W G Boulter, Mrs Boulter, Mrs Collins, Miss Armstrong, Lucy Humphries, Percy and Marion Mew, John and Annie Searle, Nora Twine, Ellen Easley, Mabel Horsell, Kate Strange, and Caroline Riddick. Robert Little was appointed as secretary. The committee was instructed to prepare a scheme and present it to a future public meeting.

The Peace Treaty was finally signed in Versailles, on Saturday 28th June 1919. The news reached Wootton Bassett between 4 and 5 o'clock. Flags were immediately hoisted, and the bells rang out a merry peal in the evening. The Town Band paraded the street playing a selection of music under the direction of Levi Easley. Everyone seemed relieved that at last peace had really come. Jolly though it must have been in town on that day, it is easy to imagine that many of Wootton Bassett's population had travelled into Swindon, to join in with the celebrations there. Swindon had begun their celebrations even before the news was confirmed, with the Great Western Railway hooters sounding out, flags fluttering everywhere, and everyone participating in the general melee of joy and thankfulness. Soon after 3.30pm the Evening Herald received the confirmation everyone was waiting for. Regent Street and Bridge Street were crowded with a merry, laughing crowd, many of them wearing red, white and blue rosettes. The Herald tells us that the mood was not quite so jubilant as on Armistice night, the enthusiasm being less spontaneous, but nevertheless, as the evening wore on, 'Swindon, which usually takes its pleasure soberly, let itself go'. Shops selling fireworks made a roaring trade, and squibs were being let off constantly throughout the evening. The rejoicing continued until midnight.

On the following Monday, a meeting was held in Wootton Bassett Town Hall to try to further the arrangements for the celebrations. They decided to give a meat tea to demobilised soldiers and sailors and to all residents over 60 years old, as well as a plain tea for all children up to 14 years. Two days later, these plans were rescinded. It was decided to postpone the Soldiers and Sailors event, and instead hold a general celebration for the town.

The Peace Celebration included a tea for residents, sports, a procession of decorated vehicles, a torchlight procession and bands. Reverend Mathias offered the use of his lawn at the vicarage in Station Road for the children's tea, and Sarah Drury offered the use of The Close for the other events. Henry and Samuel Lawrence won first prize in the Tradesmen's Turnout category of the Peace Parade.

Fig 11 - Henry and Samuel Lawrence, Peace Parade 1919, with thanks to RWB Town Hall Museum, Tony Sharp Collection.

Thanksgiving services were held at all the town's places of worship on the following Sunday. At the Primitive Methodist Chapel, the morning service was conducted by Reverend Richard Cowie and Reverend Turner from Middlesbrough, and the choir sang a special programme. At the Congregational Chapel, the services were conducted by Mr Taylor, a student from Hackney. At the Wesleyan Chapel Reverend H Perkins officiated. At the Parish Church, each service was preluded by a merry peal of bells. Impressive sermons were preached by Reverend Mathias and Reverend Knox from Bath. At the conclusion of the evening service, the National Anthem was sung.

The bell ropes, which had been getting a great deal of heavy use lately after a long period of silence, were becoming increasingly worn out and unsafe, but the Curriers Arms' landlord Sam Lawrence soon collected nearly £12 towards new ones.

The Belgians Repatriated

'Swindon's War Record' tells us that one hundred and seventeen Belgians remained in the Committee's care in January 1919. A large number of refugee families from Antwerp had already returned home from various parts of the country. Now the Belgian government decided that it was possible for all the remaining exiles to return. The Belgian government's ambitious goal was to get all the Belgian refugees home by the end of March, at a rate of 10,000 per week. Mr Basil Peto, the Repatriation Commissioner, was asked to initiate the repatriations from England, whilst in Belgium, a reception committee was to make arrangements to provide temporary accommodation in Antwerp for the returning refugees. The King of the Belgians put up a sum of 100,000f to facilitate the process.

The British government undertook to provide free transport to all Belgians who sent in their application forms by March 1st 1919. A limited amount of first class accommodation was made available on the transport vessels at a charge of £3 per head, for any Belgians who wished to pay for their own passage. The Ministry of Shipping, who had recently been engaged in evacuating British Prisoners of War from Europe, were now required to provide a regular service from London to Antwerp and from Dover to Ostend. Each refugee was given a baggage allowance of 300lb, and the War Trade Department agreed to waive the usual license required for the export of cotton, silk, wool or linen goods, provided that any such goods fell within the weight limit per head. The Ministry of Food was similarly flexible, permitting the refugees to include a reasonable amount of food, for personal use only,

[170]

to a maximum of 12lb per head, including no more than 2lb of coffee. In Swindon, the Red Cross Hospital Committee distributed the blankets left in their hands at the end of the war to the returning Belgians for comfort on their journey.

A farewell social gathering was held at Swindon Town Hall. Many members of the Committee and local supporters attended including the Mayor and Mayoress, Mrs Arnold-Forster, Mr and Mrs Ashford of Burderop, Miss Withy the secretary, and Doctor Beatty. The event included music, song, dance, and a speech by the Mayor, to which Monsieur Mommens replied, expressing his gratitude to the town on behalf of his countrymen. The last large party of 63 Belgians left Swindon in April and were waved off at the Great Western Station by the Mayor, members of the Committee and friends. In his book 'Swindon's War Record' W D Bavin tells us that only one group remained, a family of three who had been staying in Wroughton. Their home in Ypres had been devastated, and alternative accommodation was required. With their repatriation at the end of April, a chapter of history closed.[15] The Swindon Committee sold off the furniture which had been donated to Belgian refugees in 1914 or 1915 and not reclaimed by the donors. They donated the proceeds, together with the balance of funds remaining in their hands, to the Swindon Victoria Hospital. Bavin writes,

It should be stated that the demeanour and conduct of Swindon's guests throughout their long stay in the town and district were most gratifying, and gave no grounds for the complaints made in some towns. Most of the refugees came from the peasant and lower middle class, but, as regards the latter section, it is doubtful whether an equal number of English

[15] The story of the departure of the Van Rickstal family who had been staying at 164 High Street in Wootton Bassett can be found in the Town companion volume.

representatives of the class, chosen haphazard, would have displayed so much good breeding and cultivation, and they have left behind some very pleasant memories of their sojourn in the town.

Demobilisation and Dissent

Many of the folks at home found it difficult to accustom themselves to the idea that the war was over because their loved ones were not yet safe at home. The Herald reported in June 1919 that in nearly every post they were receiving letters of complaint from men who were serving abroad and were impatient to be home again. Particularly aggrieved were those men who had joined up at the outbreak of war in 1914, especially when they could see that many of those who had never served on foreign soil or had only joined up when compelled to do so, were being demobilised before them. The 1st/4th Wiltshires in Egypt were among those stranded abroad, waiting for replacements who never came, living in makeshift quarters which felt increasingly permanent. Other Wiltshiremen were detained in India because of trouble brewing on the Afghan frontier.

Some of the ex-soldiers arriving home were angered by what they found. Jobs were scarce, and women and girls had taken up many of the employment opportunities they had hoped to fill. Army pensions were insecure, the proposed 20 per cent bonus inadequate, and there was outrage at the lack of appropriate pay for men transferred to the Army Reserve. They gradually divided into two camps, the rebellious and the law-abiding. In June hundreds of discharged and disabled soldiers and sailors took part in a demonstration parade in Swindon. Their battle cry was 'We want work, not charity!' On 21st July 1919 protesters burned down a commemorative flagpole outside Swindon Town Hall with barrels of tar and petrol, and smashed windows at the police station and a number of shops. They were angry at the lavish spending on unnecessary memorials when so little was being done to relieve poverty. After three nights of rioting, the Mayor introduced a curfew, and the law-abiding faction of ex-soldiers volunteered to patrol the streets and help bring the riots under control.

The level of unemployment grew worse over the coming year, and the situation was exacerbated by the reduction of unemployment benefit, increased food prices and the depreciation of the pound. The Swindon branch of the National Federation of Discharged Sailors and Soldiers arranged another demonstration in May 1920. This time it was an orderly affair, which aimed to encourage the men of the district to support the Federation in its national and collective approaches to the Government. The first speaker, Mr F C Whitby, spoke on the distress of the district. He confirmed that on 7th May 1920 numbers in receipt of out-of-work donations (unemployment benefit) in Swindon, Cirencester, Cricklade, Malmesbury, Marlborough, Wootton Bassett, Highworth and Faringdon had reached a total of 2106 men and 54 women. One of the speakers, Mrs Noble, put the case powerfully: "If the government had made as much ado to prepare the way for peace as they had made in carrying on the war, the present-day problems of unemployment and house-shortage would not be present with us today; at least, in not such an alarming degree." She went on to say, "We want new schools, a new hospital, new houses. We want the filthy canal put right, and the roads too. Unfortunately, we have not the money to do it, and the rates of Swindon are enormously high at the present time."

Soldiers' and Sailors' Day 1919

The people of Wootton Bassett entertained their soldier and sailor heroes in magnificent style on August 9th 1919, when Fred Twine and his wife Nora Twine threw open their beautiful gardens at the Manor House for 200 guests to enjoy a sumptuous dinner on the cool and shady lawn. The day must have been a truly memorable one, and the event was blessed with glorious sunshine. The event was organised by a ladies' committee, including Nora Twine, Fanny Weston, Mrs Rich (Rebecca or Nellie), Mrs Hunt, Sarah Drury, and Isabella Armstrong, who made all the arrangements and dealt with the catering. The tables were beautifully decorated by Mrs Skinner. Most of the items on the dinner menu were donated by local folk, including two calves, a lamb, a large joint of beef, potatoes, peas, marrows, plum puddings, and a selection of 'dainties', together with a variety of alcoholic beverages, with which the company drank heartily to the health of the King, the Army and the Navy, the host, the hostess, and the ladies. There was also a silent toast in honour of those who had fallen in the war.

After dinner, everyone decamped to Harold Dale's field for a cricket match between Mr Dale's team and the Parish Council team. Mr Dale's team won by an innings. During the afternoon the Gorse Hill Prize Band played selections of music, and as the day wore on into the early evening, Madame Kingdom Difford's Concert Party, the Puritans, gave an excellent concert including chorus items, solo songs, duets and instrumental items which was greatly appreciated by the large audience. The piano was lent by the Nellie Rich. At the close of the concert, Mr Howard Horsell proposed a vote of thanks to Madame Difford and her party for their kindness in attending. Sam Lawrence's Jazz Band also played and was held to be great fun. Miss May Martin in the guise of Madame Naidu did a very brisk trade with her fortune-telling, the proceeds of which went into the funds. Later some races were held, among which the Jazz Band and Fancy Dress novelty races caused much amusement. Finally, the proceedings concluded with dancing on the lawn.

The Peace Pageant 1919

A Peace Pageant entitled "The Empire's Destiny" was held on the vicarage lawn on a Thursday in late September 1919. The pageant was organised by Lucy Humphries. The double terrace formed a stage and backdrop for the tableaux. The singing was provided by a group which included members of the Primitive Methodist Choir, and the pianist was Miss M Wallis. The principal characters in the tableaux were Britannia performed by Miss K Watts, The Past by Mrs Harvie, The Future by Nellie Rich, St George by Mr C Taylor, Brotherhood by Miss Norah Thornbury, Thrift by Miss Muriel Telling, Foresight by Miss K Fricker, Love by Miss Mabel Parke the nurse's daughter, Faith by Miss D Herring and Prayer by Miss W Heron. Other particularly popular performances were France, portrayed by Miss Brown, and The Superman. Each part was difficult but brilliantly portrayed. The scene with Future and all her children was particularly pretty, and the final tableau was very much admired. The mood was generally a joyous one, but some more sombre elements were included, in particular, the Hymn of Remembrance. Many little flags were sold by Miss K Little and Mrs R Little. The £11.3s.5d raised was given to the St Dunstan's Hostel for Blinded Soldiers and Sailors.

Armistice Day 1919

Armistice Day was specifically dedicated by King George V on 7 November 1919 as a day of remembrance for members of the armed forces who were killed during the Great War. He requested that "All locomotion should cease, so that, in perfect stillness, the thoughts of everyone may be concentrated on reverent remembrance of the glorious dead." Accordingly, the bell in Wootton Bassett was tolled for half a minute at 11am, and the King's wish for was silence observed by some of the parishioners, but not all. Perhaps the dissent in Swindon was also felt in Wootton Bassett. It was recorded with distaste that the men waiting outside the Labour Exchange did not raise their hats and that some of the traffic continued to pass. "Apparently," reported the local correspondent in the Herald, "two minutes could not be spared to think of those who had laid down their lives that we might live in peace." The Church was open to the public for silent prayer. At a large open meeting of the Men's Own Brotherhood, Mr E Tuck of Chippenham gave an address on 'Silence'. In the evening a quarter peal of Grandsire doubles were rung by members of the Wootton Bassett Guild of Bell-ringers, including O P Hewitt, Harold Ewart Flewelling, L A Wilson (conductor), E Hoare, Maurice Tucker, W G Strange, Frank Harris, and Charles Curtis, who rang the tenor bell which was to become so important in the repatriations which took place in Wootton Bassett nearly a hundred years later.

Supper for Soldiers in Wootton Bassett

In August 1920 the Committee of the Wootton Bassett Troop of Boy Scouts invited about thirty ex-servicemen who had been members of the Boy Scouts to a supper at the Manor House, hosted by Mr and Mrs Fred Twine. The event began with a stroll around the grounds. Alfred Humphries presided, supported by Howard Horsell and Richard Parsons. The ladies attended to the guests' needs with every possible care. The toast to the King was received with cheers, the National Anthem was sung, and the company toasted the health of Mr L R Bird, the District Commissioner. Mr Bird gave an interesting address on the benefits of Boy Scout training to the lads of the nation. After supper, there was an opportunity to play billiards, with music and singing, which was all much enjoyed. The Scouts produced a handwritten Roll of Honour which still hangs in their meeting hut. It lists members of the Troop who fought in the war, including both those who served and those who fell.

Dinner for Soldiers in Lydiard Tregoze

The returned soldiers of Lydiard Tregoze were invited to an evening dinner at Hook School on a Friday in January 1920, by kind invitation of Lady Bolingbroke and Edward Hiscock. The party included the Rectors D Harrison and Herbert Harrison, Captain St John, the Honourable C St John, H White, Elliott George Woolford of Hook Farm, G Parsons, and G H Ludlow. Edward Hiscock expressed his great pleasure at meeting so many of the returned men. He explained that they had postponed the dinner in hopes that more of them would be back, but some were still away. A smoking concert was held afterwards, with an excellent programme of music. The guests were waited on by ladies of the parish: Mrs Mabel White, Mrs E Woolford, the Misses Hiscock, the Misses Wheeler, A Woolford, and Ruby Gleed.

Armistice Day 1920

Armistice Day 1920 was commemorated with all due ceremony in Wootton Bassett. The flag at the Parish Church was flown at half-mast, and at 11 o'clock in the morning, the bell was solemnly tolled as a signal to engage in two minutes of prayerful silence. In the evening an impressive service was conducted by the Reverend J C S Mathias in the Parish Church. The church bells were rung both before and after the service. The service was attended by the Boy Scouts under Scoutmaster Skinner and Alfred Ricks Humphries. An offertory for the war memorial screen was held. The sermon was preached by Reverend C A Mayall, Vicar of the Parish Church of Swindon. He took for his text a portion of the 46th chapter of Isaiah, 'Remember this, and show yourselves men'. A large congregation joined in with the singing of the hymns, 'O God our help in ages past', 'Ten thousand times ten thousand', and 'How bright these glorious spirits shine'. At the Close a verse of the National Anthem was sung, the Last Post was played by F Hart and G Taylor, and William Timbrell Baxter the organist played, 'Oh rest in the Lord'.

White Chrysanthemums

On Armistice Day 1920, Rose Lawrence, the daughter of Sam Lawrence at the Curriers Arms, laid a bunch of white chrysanthemums on the Cenotaph in Whitehall, London, as a tribute to all the men of the town who fell in the war. Rose was in service in Kensington at the time. A group calling themselves 'Grateful Ones' wrote to the Herald to thank her:

May we beg a small space in your valuable paper to offer our grateful thanks to Miss Rose Lawrence (as we cannot do personally) for her kind thought in placing on the Cenotaph in Whitehall the bunch of flowers as a tribute to our brave men who lost their lives in the war. We who have lost our loved ones feel we cannot express our thanks sufficiently to her and wish now to show our gratefulness.

Fig 12 - Emily Rose Lawrence (Rose) in 1918, with thanks to John Harris.

The Saga of the German Gun

For many years a Russian gun was installed under the Town Hall in Wootton Bassett. It was a 38 pound gun, captured at Sebastopol and presented to the town by Lord Panmure. In November 1919 the Parish Council expressed the desire to acquire a similar war trophy in the form of a German field gun, as well as a smaller trophy of some kind which could be placed inside the Town Hall. It was perhaps a mistake not to canvass the town for its opinion on the matter, for things did not work out as they expected. Great excitement prevailed in Wootton Bassett on 25th February 1920 when the German gun which had been allotted to Wootton Bassett arrived in the town. Consternation grew among the gathered crowd when workmen began to remove railings from around the Town Hall to prepare a place for it to stand. The general opinion seemed to be that the scrap heap was the best place for it. Someone chalked on the gun 'Not wanted, first stop Camden's', referring to the scrap yard opposite the Manor House. Soon after 5pm, excitement mounted to fever pitch, and a number of men, later described by the Herald as "hobble-de-hoys" seized the gun, dragged it down the High Street, rolled it downhill to Skew Bridge and pulled it across a field where it was unceremoniously deposited in the brook at Hunts Mill.

Fig 13 - The German Gun in Hunts Mill, about 1919, with thanks to Royal Wootton Bassett Town Hall Museum.

This action was applauded by a Wantage man who wrote to the Herald to express his support for what had happened. The correspondent said that in Wantage Market Place, he had heard a group of labourers stood around the statue of King Alfred discussing the matter. A sturdy old Berkshireman bawled out: "Hast thee read the Swindon paper this week? The Wootton Bassett chaps have slung the German gun into the brook!" "Good," was the reply, "That's the stuff to g'ie 'em. I expect they took the tip from we Wantage chaps. Let's go and drink their health!"

Controversy over what to do next with the stranded gun became bitter and divisive, and nobody seemed to know which group was in the majority, although both claimed as much. It was suggested that the discharged soldiers and sailors should have the casting vote. The matter was hotly debated at the Annual Parish Council Meeting on

Wednesday 17th March 1920, Mr Herren presiding over a crowded attendance. Mr Kembrey sought the support of the meeting for the Council's original decision, but this was clearly not forthcoming. After a great deal of animated discussion, Mr Street moved that the parish meeting was not competent to deal with the decision and that a public meeting should be called to decide what to do. Mr Heffer seconded this, and the proposal was carried by an overwhelming majority.

As the Public Meeting commenced, Mr Street was voted to the chair. He remarked that he had not taken any side in the matter, nor expressed an opinion. He simply wished them to think over what steps they were taking because after their decision was made, it could not be altered. Mr Henry Lawrence proposed, and Mr C Edwards seconded, that the gun should not be kept. Francis Teagle asked what the legal position was, and the Chairman replied that it was not for him to say. Mr Teagle must ask the Parish Council, who brought the gun here. The motion to reject the gun was carried by an overwhelming majority, and it was decided to offer the gun for scrap by tender, and for the money so raised to be donated to the War Memorial Fund.

Despite this decision, the gun remained in the brook for many months. On November 24th 1920 the Parish Council met, Daniel Kembrey presiding, and the issue of the German gun was reopened. It was suggested that it should be raised from the brook and placed somewhere more suitable. Many members appeared to think that public feeling had altered and that they were now better disposed towards its reinstatement as a trophy, in fact, some who were involved in its disposal might even be prevailed upon to haul it back up the hill. It was decided that the Soldiers and Sailors Federation's opinion should be formally sought before any steps were taken, as they did not want to provoke any renewal of hostility or bad feeling. In December the Council duly wrote to the Federation inviting them to send representatives to meet them. However, the Federation held a meeting at the Red Lion in December 1920 to which all ex-servicemen were invited, and passed the following resolution:

> *That the Federation are of the opinion that as they were not consulted when the gun was brought to Wootton Bassett, neither do they hold themselves responsible for its present position, they leave the matter of its removal entirely to the discretion of the Parish Council.*

Snubbed by the Federation, the matter was raised again at the Parish Council meeting in January 1921, presided over by Mr Kembrey. As before, the discussion was heated. Much of the same ground was covered, but an additional problem was raised: how would the issue of the gun affect the contributions to the planned YMCA Memorial Institute in Station Road. Many members felt strongly that the gun should be removed from the parish altogether. It was eventually decided by five votes to three, that the Clerk should write to the Lord Lieutenant of the county to establish to whom the gun actually belonged.

By March no decision had been reached. The Council's prevailing feeling was still that the gun should be brought back into town and displayed somewhere appropriate. It was resolved to discuss the matter at the forthcoming annual meeting. Here it was again decided to turn the matter over to a public meeting. This took place on March 21st 1921 in the Council Schools with Mr Kembrey presiding. Mr R Little, the Clerk, read out the record of the Parish meeting's recommendations to the assembled gathering:

> *To reopen the question of the German gun on the recommendation of the Parish Council to remove it from its present position of ignominy and place it under the Town Hall, the said Council being of the opinion that such a significant monument was deserving of the best possible position,*

that posterity, and particularly the children of our brave sailors and soldiers, may view with pride and admiration one captured evidence of the pains and suffering by which liberty and freedom from German domination had been gained.

Mr Hawke asked who the gun belonged to, and Mr Kembrey read a letter from the Lord Lieutenant confirming that it belonged to the Parish Council. Mr Hawke then asked who had paid for the gun and had the cost been taken out of the rates. Mr Kembrey confirmed that it was brought voluntarily and that the rates had not been used. Mrs Little moved that the gun be placed under the Town Hall and this was seconded by James Frank Underhill. Mr Hawke made a counter proposal that as Wroughton had expressed interest in obtaining a German gun, perhaps it could be given to them. Mr Lawrence seconded this suggestion. Mr C E Street asked what would happen if the public meeting decided to dispose of the gun, but the Parish Council wanted to keep it. Mr Kembrey thought this unlikely, but if it did happen, the matter would require further consideration. Mr Hawke now withdrew his earlier suggestion to give the gun to Wroughton and said instead that the gun should be put up for tender as scrap iron and the proceeds given to the War Memorial Fund. Mr Osbourn seconded this. Mr Street was still concerned that the Parish Council needed to discuss the matter. James Underhill explained that the Parish Council were in favour of keeping the gun, and had called this meeting to decide the question. He thought that if the gun were not to be placed under the Town Hall, it should remain where it was as a memorial to those who put it there. The Chairman put Mr Hawke's proposition to scrap the gun to the vote, and it was carried by an overwhelming majority.

Some, including the editorial columnist of the Herald, thought that the decision was a travesty. He thought that what had happened to the gun was a disgrace and desecration, and that the gun should be rescued with all speed and set up in an honoured central position to remind all the residents of the sacrifices made on their behalf. The significant factor, he said, was not that this was a German gun, but that it was a captured German gun, and as such, it should stand as a symbol of freedom. In the end, the gun found its way to the front garden of a bungalow in the High Street, and there it remained for 21 years, before leaving the town for good.

The British Legion

The National Federation of Discharged and Demobilized Sailors and Soldiers was a comrades organisation founded in early 1917. It was opposed to the Review of Exceptions Act, which made it possible for people invalided out of the armed forces to be re-conscripted. Some local groups concerned themselves more with politics and others more with welfare, including simple but valuable measures such as setting up soup kitchens. The very similarly named National Association of Discharged Sailors and Soldiers was a separate organisation which campaigned for better pensions, and more opportunities for re-training. In 1920 the National Federation, the National Association and the Officers' Association met to discuss a potential merger, and this was achieved in 1921, establishing the British Legion.

A Wootton Bassett Branch of the National Federation of Discharged and Demobilized Sailors and Soldiers was operational by February 1919. James Frank Underhill of the Post Office was the first President of the Wootton Bassett Branch. Amongst the earliest events on behalf of the Federation was a concert in aid of the local branch, held in February 1919 in the Council Schools. The concert was arranged by the branch's friends in Swindon, and the stage was decorated with plants lent by Alfred Ricks Humphries. The room was packed. During the interval, Mr Whitby, the organising secretary, gave a speech outlining the objectives of the Federation and James Underhill expressed the thanks of the members, which now numbered over 60, for the support of the public. The paper reported that James Underhill was untiring in his efforts to make the concert a success.

In March several influential gentlemen in Wootton Bassett, whose names are not known, generously placed the sum of £1,500 at the disposal of the National Federation of Disabled Sailors and Soldiers for deserving cases in the County of Wiltshire. The Federation combined forces with some visiting Diocesan Missioners in June 1919, to hold an outdoor service in memory of the men of Wootton Bassett who had fallen in the war. During their visit, the missioners, Canon Farmer and Corporal Ayer, celebrated Holy Communion daily, held an outdoor service every evening near the Town Hall, and made house-to-house calls offering sympathetic counsel. The Society thanked Canon Farmer for kindly consenting to hold the service in the midst of one such busy day. The outdoor Memorial Service on Sunday afternoon attracted a large congregation, including 50 members of the Federation and some Boy Scouts. The addresses given were excellent, and it must have been a truly poignant moment when two soldiers, Private S Hart and Private Curtis, sounded the Last Post.

On the very next day, the bank holiday of June 9th 1919, a very different occasion took place when the Wootton Bassett branch of the Federation held an athletic sports event on a field lent by Fred Twine of the Manor House. The weather was perfect, and the occasion attracted a large gathering from the surrounding district. James Frank Underhill and his committee were commended for their efforts in arranging the event. Fred Twine and Hervey William White were the judges, and James Frank Underhill was the starter for the races. The many events were keenly contested and the children's sports, including a pony race won by Mr Drury's Flossie, were particularly popular. The Wootton Bassett Town Band played selections of music and also played for the dancing in the evening.

This successful event was repeated on the bank holiday in 1920, although this time it took place at the Wootton Bassett Football Ground. The weather was fine, and large numbers attended. There was a long programme of events including a wide variety of races, novelty races and pony races, and Levi Easley led the Town Band in a selection of music throughout the afternoon. One of the favourite events was a bun-eating competition for boys, in which buns smothered with treacle were tied to a piece of string, and the boys had their hands tied behind them. This event evoked howls of laughter from all who watched. The winners, who ate theirs first, were W Crombie, H Inkpen, A Harper and [?] Sandall. Another popular event was a hotly contested tug-of-war with opposing teams from Wootton Bassett and Purton. Wootton Bassett, captained by Sam Lawrence, emerged victorious on the last of three pulls.

The Federation held elections in December 1920 to select officers for the following year. The President was Mr E Wallis, Vice President Mr A Twine, the Treasurer Mr G Read and the Honorary Secretary Mr H Trow. The committee members were Mr P Mew, Mr H Lawrence, Mr J Hawe, Mr F Bushell, Mr A H Hunt, Mr J Lane, Mr H L Reeves, Mr B Choules, Mr S Foss, and Mr J Hawe. The branch announced that they had a membership of 60, and a bank balance of about £40. They had helped a number of deserving cases locally, to the tune of £20 in total. The members resolved to renew their efforts to recruit more members and to hold a dinner in the near future. In 1921 the Wootton Bassett branch of the Federation was based at 17 High Street. The President was Mr Wallis, the Treasurer Mr Choules, and the Secretary Mr A J Gibbs. In March 1921 there were over 70 members.

After the formation of the British Legion in 1921, the local branch of the Federation evolved to become the Wootton Bassett and District branch of the British Legion. The first annual meeting of the branch took place on January 2nd 1922. For many years the British Legion in Wootton Bassett had no premises of their own, so this meeting was held at their temporary headquarters at the Crown Hotel. The President, Mr E Wallis, took the Chair, supported by Vice President Mr A Twine. Mr Wallis was re-elected for the following year. The assistant secretary announced that 15 new members had joined, and hopes were expressed for a more successful year ahead. A motion was passed to establish a Sick and Loan Society for members, and a small sub-committee was established to see this through.

In March 1925 the President Mr H Wallis announced that they had finally succeeded in finding premises for the branch: a private house next door to the Primitive Methodist Church. The name was not decided but was likely to be "The British Legion Club and Institute". A considerable sum was invested in carrying out the necessary alterations. There was a commodious room with a bar and ample accommodation for a live-in steward. The land at the rear was earmarked for an extension in due course. The new club for the 'old warriors' opened on Saturday, 13th June 1925. Major Calley was invited to perform the opening ceremony, but he was unable to attend, so no official opening took place.

The Club became a popular venue. It hosted entertainments such as a visit from the A1 Concert Party from Swindon in September 1926, and during the following decade, it was an active member of the local darts and skittles leagues. The steward of the Club until April 1931 was Mr W Godwin, who was then succeeded by Mr Curley, formerly of Highworth. The Honorary Secretary in 1930 was Mr G E Franklin.

In March 1936 the British Legion announced that they were planning to move from the existing club premises and purchase the building known as the 'gymnasium' in Sparrow Lane from the owner, Lucy Humphries, for the purpose of converting it into a headquarters. The purchase money was to be raised by the members and by public subscription, and the necessary renovation was to be carried out by the members voluntarily. During March and April 1936 the "High Street Club" was advertising for a residential stewardess; the Legion had moved out. In October 1936 the British Legion presented their first annual report in their new hall, stating that more than £30 had been given to needy cases and five jobs were found for ex-servicemen. The President at that time was General John Hartman Morgan of Wood Street.

In 1937 Lucy Humphries made a Conveyance with three Trustees of the local British Legion by which Deed she sold the little hall in Sparrow Lane to the Wootton Bassett Branch of the British Legion for £20. The conveyance stated that the Branch's Trustees "may sell the premises at such time and in such manner as they think fit". The British Legion remained in Sparrow Lane until they sold it in 2004.

War Graves

Graves after the Great War

The work of finding field burials, identification of remains, and recording and photographing them, was a massive undertaking, hampered by the demobilisation of troops, and a lack of photographers and suitable motor vehicles. By May 1919, 373,351 graves had been identified and registered in France and Belgium, and 154,823 other burials, such as those which could not be found, or those which had been destroyed by shellfire, had been registered.

Initially, the War Office announced that it was not possible to give general permission to visit graves, particularly in closed areas where efforts were being made to concentrate isolated graves in battlefield sites into groups. It was possible to visit registered graves by special permit in very particular situations, such as when relatives from Australia or Canada were only temporarily in Europe. Even then, visits were difficult to arrange due to a shortage of suitable transport and accommodation. Unfortunately, we do not know whether any local families visited the graves of their loved ones abroad during the difficult months which followed the war. I have only found one man connected with Wootton Bassett who was engaged on this tragic and painstaking work: Private David Arthur Jefferies who was born in Coxstalls in 1861 and served in 126 Labour Company (692272).[16]

---

[16] For David Jefferies' story, see Coxstalls unknown addresses in the Town companion volume.

CWGC Graves in Wootton Bassett Cemetery

In the Cemetery, you will find three Commonwealth war graves from World War I and four from World War II. The WW1 graves are those of Edgar James Wright, Albert Edmonds, and William Arthur Westmacott.

War Memorials

Wootton Bassett Screen, Tablet, and Roll of Honour

At the first meeting of the newly elected Parochial Church Council, held in the vestry in early May 1920 it was unanimously decided to place a war memorial tablet in the parish church. Reverend Mathias presided with Mr Isaac Watts as Vice Chairman and John Sanders Searle as secretary. A discussion revealed that a few parishioners had expressed a preference for the memorial to be put up in the churchyard, but having regard to possible legal and other difficulties that might arise, it was resolved to adhere to the expressed wishes of both the Easter vestry and the meeting of the church electors, and to erect the memorial within the church. The first appeal for subscriptions was made during the Sunday 9th May service, and a subscription list was arranged for. Collections were made at subsequent church services. A poster dated 18th December 1920 was printed by Riddick, advertising a vestry meeting at 6pm on Thursday 23rd December in the vestry room, to approve an application for a faculty to erect a memorial screen and tablet in the parish church. A further collection was made at the Christmas Day services of 1920.

The task of collecting names for the church memorial fell to John Sanders Searle, Master of the Church Schools. In a letter to Mr Dale dated 17th March 1921 he enclosed a list of names for the tablet, neatly written in upper and lower case for total clarity, saying that they had all been verified by relatives and friends, so they should be correct. His letter contains some interesting ancillary notes:

Albert Edmonds' father refused information desired, but Church Parochial Council meeting on March 2nd it was stated that the family wished the name to appear, so I applied to Mrs Alden and got particulars through her. The name of Jesse Lawrence I am told is on the

Hook Memorial. His father in Swindon gave me particulars before I knew of this. Some Hunts are not in alphabetical order. Alfred Reginald Hunt and Clarence Joseph Hunt are brothers, and so are Archibald H Hunt and G Seymour Hunt. I have several interesting particulars concerning each of the fallen: their rank, regiment, age, date and place of death. What do you say to placing these in a frame near the Memorial? It would be a useful record and might give satisfaction and comfort to the relatives concerned - but this is only a suggestion.

In a postscript he added:

Augustus M Sargent and William H Twine were 2nd Lieutenants. Commissioned rank is stated on some memorials.

The Parochial Church Council wrote to all interested parties inviting them to the unveiling service and requesting estimated numbers. They announced that Major-General Calley would unveil the screen and that Archdeacon Bodington would dedicate it. A J Gibbs, Secretary of the Wootton Bassett branch of the Federation of Discharged Soldiers and Sailors, replied saying that they had discussed the matter at a meeting at 17 High Street on 30th May 1921 and that about seventy members would like to attend the Church as a body.

The Parish Council read out the invitation at their meeting, and Mr Page (probably John Thomas Page) moved that they should accept and attend as a body. This was seconded by Mr Rich and carried unanimously. Robert Little replied to the Church Council on their behalf saying that the general feeling in the Council was an earnest desire to be present, and that probably 13 of the Council members would attend. Two sent their apologies: Mr E G Strange said that he appreciated the invitation very highly but greatly regretted that he could not attend due to a prior commitment, believed to be a preaching duty; the other was unnamed.

The completed tablet and screen were unveiled in Wootton Bassett Church on Sunday, 5th June 1921. It consists of a splendid oak belfry screen with eighteen leaded glass panels. Beside this was a brass tablet, with an oak frame, made by W H Sheppard of Frome. The screen and tablet were acknowledged to be beautiful specimens of the craftsman's art and made a great improvement to the belfry entrance to the church. The tablet reads:

This screen was erected to the glory of God and in honoured memory of those men of this parish who made the supreme sacrifice in the Great War 1914-1918

G Angelinetta

O E Angelinetta

A Beazley

H Beazley

C Blanchett

A Brown

B Brown

H Brown

W E Burchell

E S Cox

A Edmonds

S F Foster

H Gibbs

J C B Gibbs

T E Gibson

W T H Harris

S Hart

E Helps

A E Hewer

J Hird

C H Hughes

A R Hunt

C J Hunt

A H Hunt

G S Hunt

H J Hunt

L F J Hunt

R Hunt

C Lovelock

G E Lovelock

H J Merrett

S A Merrett

R C Painter

A J Peaple

R C Rowe

W J Sainsbury

A M Sargent

G Sawyer

H S Street

L H G Taylor

A Twine

A S Twine

W H Twine

F Watts

W A Westmacott

E J Wright

The men were very good unto us, and we were not hurt. They were a wall unto us both by night and day. 1 Sam XXV, 15 16.

Fig 14 - St Bartholomew's Parish Church Memorial Screen and Tablet, photographed by Sheridan Parsons 2014.

For the dedication service, the church was packed to its utmost capacity. The Boy Scouts and Cubs under Scoutmaster Skinner were seated in the Lady Chapel to the right of the chancel, the front right pews were occupied by the Council with members of the Discharged Soldiers and Sailors behind them, and the relatives of the deceased were allocated the back right pews with the best view of the belfry screen and tablet. The service, which was stately and beautiful in every way, opened with the hymn, 'Let saints on earth', followed by the lesson which was read by the Reverend Mathias. Isaac Watts, the people's warden, invited General Calley, standing on the chancel step, to unveil the screen on behalf of the congregation. General Calley delivered a short address in which he thanked the people of Wootton Bassett for allowing him to pay tribute to the men of the parish.

It was seven years ago that the terrible cloud hung over the world. It was my duty and honour to come to Wootton Bassett to ask men to join the colours, and I surely need not tell you that I felt it to be a great responsibility. The men whose names are on the tablet sacrificed their lives for our honour and safety, and beautiful as that screen is, it is not worthy of the men. I do not mean to say that it is at all mean, but if it were the most beautiful memorial man could turn out, it would not be worthy. Can you not raise a living memorial by helping to restore peace and goodwill? Do your best to promote peace; offer a kindly hand to someone else and refuse to join in petty quarrels. Let that be the memorial for the deeds that have been achieved.

The wardens and clergy then proceeded to the belfry with General Calley, who unveiled the memorial with the words:

In the name of the congregation and people of Wootton Bassett, I unveil this memorial screen and tablet to our brothers who gave their lives in defence of King and country, for our safety, and in the cause of freedom and justice. I now ask that this memorial may be dedicated to the Glory of God.

Archdeacon Bodington of Calne then dedicated the memorial with the words:

To the honour and glory of Almighty God, in the faith of a joyful resurrection, and looking for the mercy of our Lord Jesus Christ, we dedicate this screen and tablet in loving memory of His servants, men of this parish, who gave their lives for King and country in this Great War. In the name of the Father, and of the Son, and of the Holy Ghost. Amen.

As the procession returned to the chancel the congregation sang, 'O Valiant Hearts'. The Archdeacon then gave an address.

Let me, like General Calley, thank you for the great honour you have done me by asking me to come and pay my humble tribute to the men who gave their all, and, with regard to that tribute, let me associate myself with his moving and touching words. Why is it that these men are spoken of as saints? The word 'saint' in the bible means a consecrated man, and just because these men sacrificed themselves without thinking they were doing anything great, they were lifted up on the Cross with Christ. We think of them as saints because they were consecrated to do a great deed. When those men passed beyond the veil, leaving their bodies on the other side, they must see a new vision, and what they thought to be great things on earth would seem small to them there, and what seemed but small here would be great things there. The horrors of the last few years have shattered the faith of many. I do not want anyone to be unreal, none of us is what could be called a saint, but man is very little without faith. I ask you to see that you have faith in something and to exercise that faith. If you have only a fragment of faith, God will make it grow.

After the address, Rudyard Kipling's Recessional was sung. The Archdeacon then pronounced the Blessing. The Last Post was then sounded, followed by two minutes' silence. The Reveille then rang out, and the congregation joined together to sing the National Anthem. The Nunc Dimittis was chanted as the procession made its way to the belfry. It was said that the Choir, led by Mr Marchant, acquitted themselves admirably. Finally, the organist, William Timbrell Baxter, played Chopin's March Funebre as the congregation left the Church. The seven collection points arranged around the Church raised £9 1s for the memorial fund.

On the Sunday afternoon of 26th April 1925, an addition to the belfry screen in the church was dedicated with a service. No addition to the screen is apparent, and no names were added to the original tablet, so I am still looking for evidence of the nature of this addition. It may possibly refer to the top part of the belfry screen, above the eight leaded glass panels, or it may refer to Mr Searle's Roll of Honour. The afternoon's proceedings began with a march to the Church led by the Wootton Bassett Progressive Band. There was a large congregation including many ex-servicemen directed by Mr Godwin and Mr Mullard, two members of a newly formed Buffaloes Lodge, the Boy Scouts led by Mr G E Franklin, the Girl Guides under Lieutenant Mabel Parke, and the VAD nurses. The service was an impressive one, conducted by Reverend Mathias and assisted by the curate Reverend F T Pocock. It began with the hymn "Let saints on earth in concert sing". Mr Searle read the lesson, then the congregation sang "O God of Jacob by whose hand". Isaac Watts then invited the Reverend A L Scott of Derry Hill, in his capacity as Rural Dean, to unveil and dedicate the completed memorial.

Happily Mr Searle's excellent suggestion for a Roll of Honour was implemented, and was of great help in the early stages of researching this book. This framed list of names, ages and particulars of death was originally mounted on the opposite side of the screen. This is not currently on display.

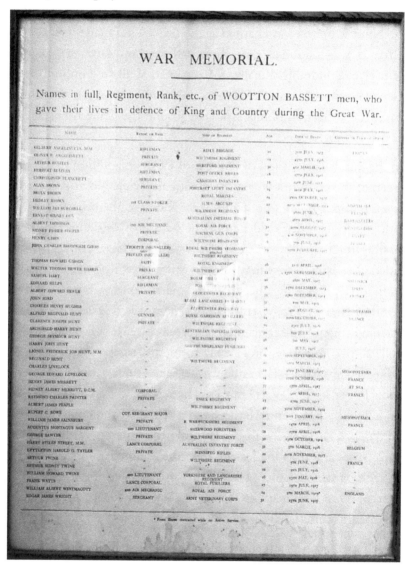

Fig 15 - Mr Searle's Roll of Honour

The Red Triangle Memorial Institute

The Parish Council held themselves responsible for creating a public non-denominational War Memorial for the town, and by March 1919 they were frequently preoccupied with a discussion of the form which this should take. The Council proposed two options, a tablet bearing the names of all the sailors and soldiers, to be placed at the Town Hall, or a similar public location, or alternatively a recreation ground. At the Annual Parish Meeting on Monday 17th March 1919, the matter was discussed with great animation. The idea of a recreation field had been on the Council's minds for a considerable time, but funding had always been the stumbling block. James Frank Underhill arrived at the meeting with positive news, that Mr R Parsons of Hunt Mill Farm wished to promote a memorial to our fallen soldiers and sailors, and had generously offered to pay any balance of the purchase money for a recreation field which could not be raised by voluntary contributions. Mr Parsons felt that the field known as The Close, opposite the Police Station, was the only field worth procuring, so his offer was limited to that field alone. The Council had already made some efforts to purchase The Close. A deputation had met with a representative of the owner, Mrs Fernie, but to no avail. James Underhill believed that Mrs Fernie's blank refusal to sell was based mostly upon sentiment.

There was a brief discussion of alternative sites, the favourite being Ernest Camden's field opposite the Manor House at the other end of the High Street. The owner, Fred Twine, had already been approached by the Council. He was willing to sell but wished to retain the strip of land nearest to the main road, where he intended to build in the future. James Underhill stressed that if this field was chosen, Mr Parsons' offer to support the purchase would not apply. He warned the meeting that the purchase of Mr Twine's field would be very costly, and that compulsory purchase would be an expensive option, and might not succeed despite the outlay. Despite some misgivings, the members agreed that The Close was the best site. They called upon the Council to make efforts to purchase The Close from its owner, Mrs Fernie, voluntarily if possible, but if necessary by such compulsory powers as the law permitted.

Early in May 1919, the Parish Council revisited the matter, and in accordance with the agreement made in March, the members resolved to make another effort to purchase The Close by voluntary arrangement. Messrs Underhill, P Leighfield, and E Boulter were appointed to seek a further interview with Mrs Fernie. At the end of the month, the Council heard that the deputation had been unsuccessful. A new group was now appointed to meet with Mr Parsons, to consult him on a few points before attempting the compulsory purchase of the land. In the meantime, the question of the provision of any other memorial to those who served in the war was deferred.

A special meeting of the Parish Council was held on Wednesday, June 18th 1919. All efforts to obtain the Close voluntarily had failed, so the Council unanimously resolved to petition the County Council to compel Mrs Fernie to sell the Close to the Council. The public enquiry took place in October 1919 at the Town Hall. The Clerk to the Council, Robert Little, gave a history of the efforts already made to purchase the field. Mr Herron chairman of the Council, Mr Kembrey Vice Chairman, James Underhill, and others, gave evidence to support the application for compulsory purchase, while local solicitor Harold Dale spoke on behalf of Mrs Fernie. Mr Dale questioned whether the Council had pursued opportunities to obtain alternative land. The Council said that the Close site had always been their favourite option, although they had on other occasions made attempts to secure some less favoured sites as a makeshift measure. Mr Dale considered that there were several other suitable fields available. He also called two auctioneers and valuers, Mr Mundy of Trowbridge, and Mr Armstrong, to show that the amenities of Mrs Fernie's house on the High Street, and those of one other house, both of which enjoyed access to the Close and rights of way over it, would be seriously prejudiced by the loss of the field. The Commissioner, Mr A M Dunne KC, viewed the Close before the hearing and heard the evidence with great patience. His report was awaited with some anxiety, presumably on both sides of the case. The decision was finally made that the Close could not be used, and the scheme fell through.

The Council suggested that the public should be invited to propose an alternative scheme, such as a tablet at the Town Hall, or some other suitable place. They resolved to put the matter on the agenda for the next annual parish meeting in March. At this meeting, a lively discussion led to the decision to create a memorial reading room and institute and to leave the arrangements for this in the hands of the Parish Council. In late August 1920, a public meeting was held in the Council Schoolroom to consider what next steps should be taken. Mr Kembrey, presiding, explained that the committee had made enquiries into the cost of erecting an institute on the Parish Council's land in Station Road. They had also looked into purchasing the Royal Oak Hotel, which had been closed for some time, and adapting it to their needs. Unfortunately, the Council considered the cost of both schemes to be beyond the resources of the Parish, even using the most moderate estimates. They were unable to recommend anything beyond a Memorial Tablet or Roll of Honour. Mr Dale mentioned that this was being already planned for the Parish Church. There was a suggestion that in contrast to the Church's memorial, theirs could be placed by the public highway, in full view of all, but Mr Wallis reflected that after the treatment of the German gun it would be tempting fate to place anything destructible by the roadside. He further remarked that unless the public did something quickly, the Soldiers' Federation would doubtless take the matter in hand. After a desultory discussion it was decided that with only a meagre attendance at the meeting, nothing important could be decided that day.

A month later another meeting was held in the Council Schoolroom to press towards a decision. Again Mr Kembrey presided over a scanty attendance. The idea of an institute was proposed by Mr Heffer, and this was supported by Mr Read, Mr Mew, and Mr Mitchell. Mr Trow felt that opinion was still too much divided to undertake so large a project. Some people, he said, were unwilling to assist until the German gun was brought back and placed in position. Church people could not be expected to help, as they were busy arranging a memorial of their own. He proposed that a memorial could be erected on the piece of ground at the approach to the cemetery, but this found no seconder. Mr Heffer proposed that a committee of five be established, with power to add more, to take the matter in hand. This was unanimously agreed, and Mr Kembrey, Mr Heffer, Mr Page (probably John Thomas Page), Mr Mew, and Mr Read were appointed.

By November 1920 the area secretary of the YMCA, Mr Neale, who had spent much time in France with the Association, offered the town a former YMCA hut to use as an Institute. A public meeting was swiftly convened at the Council Schools to decide whether to accept the gift. This time there was a fairly good attendance. Mr Kembrey, in the chair, presented an update on the work of the War Memorial Committee. Mr Neale then stepped forward. He said that the YMCA had been dedicated to improving rural life for many years. Nothing would please him more than to have a hut used as a war memorial, and he felt sure that if he could ask those who had fallen what they would want, they would surely request something that would be for the betterment of the people. He then explained the conditions of the gift, which were very specific. The building itself would be entirely free, but the town would need to pay for dismantling, transport, re-erection and furnishing. The Institute would need to be vested in four trustees; there should be a management committee of twelve with four officers, and the local YMCA secretary would be required to be an ex-officio member. It should be called the Red Triangle Hut or Club, with an additional name if desired. The red triangle was very familiar as the logo of the YMCA. Persons over 16 years of age would be eligible for membership of the Club. James Underhill asked Mr Neale where the hut was currently, and what the transport would cost. Mr Neale explained that it was on Salisbury Plain, and the cost of haulage would be around £200, but ultimately this would depend on the weather. Dates could be arranged to suit the committee's convenience. James Underhill proposed that the offer should be accepted, Mr Page (probably John Thomas Page) seconded, and it was carried unanimously.

A special meeting of the Parish Council took place on the following Monday, Mr Kembrey presiding. The discussion was earnest. It was unanimously resolved to place the hut on the Council's land opposite the vicarage in Station Road, where the Memorial Hall car park is today. The council stressed that they could not contribute anything from the rates towards the expenses of the erection, management or upkeep of the hut. The process of fundraising could now begin in earnest. Money was raised through dances, whist drives, entertainments, and other collections. The Wootton Bassett branch of the Discharged Sailors' and Soldiers' Federation held a meeting at the Red Lion in December 1920 to which all ex-servicemen were invited. They decided that a piece of furniture should be purchased and presented to the memorial hut, but that it must remain the property of the ex-servicemen.

By December 1921 the shell of the building had been erected, and the interior was nearing completion. The onerous conditions imposed by the YMCA had been moderated with assistance from Mr F Heffer, acting as the YMCA's honorary secretary. The Secretary of the War Memorial Committee announced that £334 had been collected and £306 spent, leaving a balance of £28. The original nineteen members of the committee were re-elected. Mr Tuck and Mr J Gibbs were elected as representatives of the British Legion in the place of two members who had resigned. Mr F Heffer was appointed Honorary Secretary and Mr Parsons as Honorary Treasurer. One of the YMCA conditions which persisted was that the title Red Triangle should be included in the name of the hut. After considerable discussion, it was unanimously agreed that the hut should be named 'The Wootton Bassett Red Triangle Memorial Institute'. It was decided that Mrs Brown of the Cross Keys, mother of three of the fallen, should be invited to open the building. Mr Kembrey thanked the British Legion for donating a piano to the Institute, and he expressed his gratitude to the builders who had laid the foundation and to everyone else who had given assistance. Mr Boulter asked what would be done about subscriptions, and Mr Kembrey replied that the committee had not yet discussed the matter but that they would try to keep subscriptions as low as possible. The entertainments to be held in the Institute would also raise funds for its upkeep.

The opening took place on Thursday, January 19th 1922 between 2.30pm and 3pm. The event attracted a large crowd, although apologies were received from some hoped-for invited guests including Major and Mrs Buxton, Major-General Calley, Colonel H C Theobald, Mrs Arnold-Forster, Mr R A Norman (Divisional Council of the YMCA), Mr J Sadler, Mr Ward of Purton, and Mr Shaw of Purton. Mrs Brown unlocked the door and declared the hut open, saying that she hoped that it would be the means of bringing great enjoyment to those who made use of it. Those gathered outside now flocked in. Thankfully the hut was large enough to accommodate the 300 guests. A dedication service was conducted by Reverend Mathias, Reverend King, and Reverend Richard Cowie. Those assembled sang 'Onward Christian soldiers', then Reverend King read Psalm 124, and Reverend Richard Cowie offered up a prayer. The vicar, Reverend Mathias, then dedicated the hut with the words:

> *To the memory of those from Wootton Bassett who in the Great War laid down their lives for King and country, we dedicate this hut, with the earnest prayer that it shall be made use of for the good of this town in healthy recreation and enjoyment. God grant this.*

He then said that the hut provided an opportunity to brighten the life of the people of Wootton Bassett, offer social enjoyment, contribute to the betterment of their fellow men and help them forward.

Mr Kembrey, presiding, gave a speech detailing the progress of the movement which had led to that day. Between September 23rd 1920 and December 31st 1921 £330 had been raised; £110 by donations, £35 by a house to house collection, £65 by dances, £90 by whist drives, and £30 by concerts. £291 of this had been paid out, but there were other expenses to be met, and donations would still be welcome. The ex-soldiers and sailors of the town, through the British Legion, had provided them with a piano and a table. They hoped in time to be able to add a reading room, a billiard room, a games room, and a kitchen.

On the evening of the opening, the mood was much more light-hearted. 276 guests enjoyed a social event at the Institute, supervised by a committee of ladies which had formed for the purpose. Henry Weston served as Chairman for the night. There was a high-class musical programme with a number of vocal solos, comic songs, a duologue, recitations, and stories. The room had been charmingly decorated, and everyone had a jolly time.

The present Memorial Hall is a few metres further down Station Road, and the YMCA is no longer involved. Nevertheless, it is still a wonderful hub for social and cultural events of all kinds. Mrs Brown would probably approve.

Wootton Bassett High Street War Memorial

For many years Wootton Bassett had no war memorial in the High Street. Disappointed by this omission, former mayor and Royal British Legion stalwart Ken Scott, a D-Day veteran, made a cardboard and papier-mâché Cenotaph as a centrepiece for remembrance events.[17]

Fig 16 - Members of the British Legion with Wootton Bassett's makeshift War Memorial

---

[17] Ken Scott was also responsible for creating the Remembrance Garden in the Cemetery.

Members of the British Legion gathered at this makeshift cenotaph until 1997. When a 14-year-old Army cadet, Jai Cunningham, had to lay her Armistice Day wreath at this well-meaning but somewhat absurd memorial, she was adamant that it wasn't good enough. On her initiative, a competition was launched to design a permanent memorial, and this was won by 15-year-old Alan Wilson. The design would show the world held in four hands and would illustrate the places where the British had been engaged in conflict. By 2002, £30,000 had been raised, and the town was ready to build its new memorial. The globe was cast in bronze, and a special chemical process was used to make the oceans of the globe appear blue. The War Memorial was officially dedicated in October 2004.

There is currently an error on the War Memorial. Edward Helps should read Edwin Helps. This has resulted from the continued duplication of an old mistake, perhaps arising because Edwin was known to friends and family as Ted. This error has been confirmed both by research evidence and by the testament of his grandson, but despite numerous requests to the Town Council, it has never been corrected.

The War Memorial later became well known as a symbol of the town's involvement in the repatriations. On 29th January 2010 The Prince of Wales and Camilla, Duchess of Cornwall each laid wreaths at the war memorial during a ceremony to dedicate a new flagpole. The occasion, just hours after a repatriation through the town, was marked by bitter winds and a sharp blizzard.

Fig 17 - Prince Charles and Camilla, Duchess of Cornwall, laying a wreath at the War Memorial in 2010, photographed by Mike Parsons

Hook War Memorial

At a Parish Meeting at Lydiard Tregoze on March 17th 1919 the issue of a permanent war memorial to men of the parish who had made the supreme sacrifice was raised. The members decided that, as this meeting was very small, they would call another public meeting at Hook village school on the following Monday week, specifically to deal with this issue, and hopefully to make a definite decision and take steps to put it into effect. A committee was formed to drive forward the plans for a memorial, comprising Reverend Alexander Herbert Harrison, Miss Phillips, Frederick Leighton, Mr A Snow, Mr F Rumming, Edward Hiscock, Mr J H Cole, Mr P Skull, Mr J Love, Mr E Thompson, and Hervey William White.

In due course, the War Memorial was built on the junction of the Wootton Bassett to Purton road and Hook Street. On the afternoon of Saturday, December 4th 1920, a party of local ex-servicemen, relatives of the fallen, members of the committee, and schoolchildren assembled at the school and marched to the site of the memorial, where a large number of people attended the unveiling. The service began with the singing of the hymns 'Fight the good fight' and 'O God our help in ages past'. Prayers and addresses were given by Reverend Alexander Herbert Harrison from Lydiard Tregoze, and Reverend Richard Cowie of Wootton Bassett. Reverend Harrison expressed his admiration for the wonderful spirit of sacrifice displayed by those who had given their lives for their country, and his sorrow for the grieving relatives. Next, Viscount Bolingbroke, who was to unveil the memorial, gave a speech. He said they were met to do honour to the memory of the men of the parish who courageously answered the challenge of the sword jangling militarists of Europe. In sacrificing their lives, these men had contributed nobly to a common effort to save the world from destruction. He went on,

It is with feelings of admiration and respect that I unveil this Memorial to the men of Lydiard Tregoze, who fought a good fight and died an illustrious death.

The Memorial was described in contemporary accounts as a handsome shrine, nearly twelve feet tall, and surmounted by a small cross, with a commanding view across rolling meadows and downlands stretching for miles. It was made from several grades of granite and was built by Messrs Webb and Sons of Chippenham.

Reverend Harrison performed a dedication, and then all present joined in singing 'Abide with me'. After this, Reverend Richard Cowie gave an address extolling the qualities of the British soldier. He concluded:

This Memorial is not to perpetuate the spirit of militarism; it stands for something quite the reverse. These men went out to kill militarism, and let us hope that those who were spared will learn something of the lesson. Let us see to it that the peace we have secured is a peace of goodwill; let us bury the hatchet of hatred, and let us nurture the spirit of brotherliness, of charity, and of mutual trust and esteem.

The service ended with the sounding of the last post and the singing of the National Anthem.

The memorial reads:

To the glory of God, and in memory of the men of Lydiard Tregoze who made the supreme sacrifice in the Great War 1914-18.

Serjt Ernest Arthur Townsend

Pte Reginald Skull DCM

Pte Henry Frank Porter

Pte Percival Edge Smart

Pte Edward David Embling

Pte Charles Barnes

Pte Victor Reuben Newman

Pte Frank Curtis Webb

Pte Wilfred John Parrott

Pte Thomas Jesse Laurence (sic)

Pte John Thomas Titcombe

Fig 18 - Lydiard Tregoze War Memorial at Hook, photographed by Sheridan Parsons 2014.

St Mary's Church Memorial Book

The Roll of Honour in St Mary's Church, Lydiard Tregoze, is a beautifully illuminated book, kept in a display case in the church. The men are written into the Roll of Honour in the order in which they enlisted or were embodied. The names of men who died during the Great War are inscribed in gold leaf. Men who survived are written in black ink. Where known, each listing also includes their regiment, their date and place of their death, and any decorations they received.

The Roll of Honour reads:

Saint Mary the Virgin Lydiard Tregoz. Of the Parish of Lydiard Tregoz in the County of Wilts, these served the King in the years of our Lord 1914 - 1919. As dying and behold we live.

August 1914

Private Richard Titcombe Reserve, 2nd Wilts. R.

Private William John Woodward 1st Wilts Reg.

Private Frederick Thomas Strange 4th Dragoon Guards

Private Mark Tombs Sth. Wales Borderers

Private Francis George Howard Roy. Field Artillery

Private Algernon Edwin Love R. Army Med. Corps

Private William John Morse 1st Wiltshire Reg.

Private Edward Cecil Sawyer Roy. Field Artillery

Private Bertie Henry Newman 1st Wiltshire Reg.

Private John Theodore Colledge Gloucestersh. Yeo.

Private Howard James Smart 1st Wiltshire Reg. - Killed, March 1915, Neuve-Chapelle. (this was recorded incorrectly, as he was not killed, but a POW).

Private Egbert Daniel Porter Roy. Field Artillery

Private Sidney John Porter 5th Wiltshire Reg.

August Major Mervyn Nevil Arnold-Forster M.C. Grenadier Guards

August Lieut. Hugh Christopher Arnold-Forster Royal Navy

September 1914

Gunner Thomas Tombs Roy. Field Artillery

Private Frederick Hatter 7th Wiltshire Reg.

Private Percival Edge Smart 2nd Wiltshire Reg.

Driver George Charles Embling Roy. Field Artillery

Private Frank Ind 7th Wiltshire Reg.

Sergeant Ernest Arthur Townsend 2nd Wiltshire Reg. - Killed, 12 March 1915, Buried near Chapelle.

Private John Thomas Titcombe Royal Fusiliers - Killed, 17 August 1915, Dardanelles.

Driver Albert Noon Roy. Field Artillery Killed, Salonika, (recorded incorrectly as Albert, he was Alfred James, died 24th April 1917)

Private Jesse Lawrence R. Munster Fusiliers - Killed in action, Dardanelles.

October 1914

Private Henry Frank Porter 2nd Wiltshire Reg. - Killed, June 1915.

November 1914

Lt.-Comr. William Edward Arnold-Forster Royal Naval Vol. Res.

Captain Henry Mildmay St.John Gloucester Reg.

December 1914

Driver Albert James Wise Roy. Field Artillery

Private Edward James Webb Roy. Wiltshire Yeo.

Seaman Walter Titcombe R.M.S. Collingwood

January 1915

Driver Arthur Morse Roy. Field Artillery

February 1915

Private Reginald Skull, D.C.M. 2nd Wiltshire Reg. - Killed, 9 April 1917, Buried Neuville Vitase Cemetery, France.

Trooper Herbert John Crew Roy. Wiltshire Yeo.

Signaller Edward Alec Kinch Roy. Field Artillery

Private Charles Barnes 5th Wiltshire Reg. - Killed, 18 October 1915, Dardanelles.

March 1915

Private Edward David Embling 5th Wiltshire Reg. - Died of Fever, Persian Gulf.

April 1915

Corporal Alfred John Strange Rifle Brigade

Private Victor Reuben Newman 9th R. Warwicks. R. - Killed, 3rd September.

May 1915

Gunner Albert Victor George Bezzant Roy. Field Artillery

Lieutenant Charles Reginald St.John 7th Somerset Lt. Inf.

June 1915

Gunner Alfred George Newman Roy. Garrison Art.

Private Ernest John Painter New Zealand Reg.

Captain John Anthony Arnold-Forster Roy. Field Artillery

Driver William Noon Roy. Field Artillery

August 1915

Wilfred John Parrott Machine Gun Corps - Died in France, 22 February 1919 (recorded incorrectly as Wilfred - he was William)

October 1915

Gunner Ernest Thomas Skull Roy. Field Artillery D.C.M., M.S.M.

November 1915

Private Ernest James Titcombe 1st Wiltshire Reg.

Private Alfred John Embling 1st Wiltshire Reg.

Private Joseph Hatter 1st Wiltshire Reg.

December 1915

Private John Ernest Strange 1st Wiltshire Reg.

December Gunner Bertie Thale Strange Royal Marine Artillery

January 1916

Private Victor Edward North Woodward 1st Wiltshire Reg.

Driver Sidney Charles Pinnegar Roy. Field Artillery

Gunner Arthur Hubert Sawyer

March 1916

Private Snowdon Henry Love Australian Imp. F.

Private Edward John Titcombe Roy. Berkshire Reg.

Gunner Alfred Rudler Roy. Garrison Art.

April 1916

Corporal Stanley Painter Worcestershire Reg.

Private George Henry Cowley Army Service Corps

May 1916

Private Wilfred Sidney Tanner 48th Aust. Imp. F.

Gunner Henry William Soule Roy. Field Artillery

June 1916

Private William Titcombe Durham Lt. Inf. - Killed, 28 March 1918, France.

2nd Lieut. Frederick William Leighton Royal Engineers

Private Alfred Henry Curtis 2nd Worcester. R.

September 1916

Private Francis Tom Titcombe 10th D. of Wellington's R.

December 1916

Private William James Bezzant 9th Wiltshire Reg.

January 1917

Private Rawleigh Charles Webb Australian Imp. Fce.

Captain Herbert Melville Leighton 8th Persian Rifles

March 1917

Private Gordon James Love The Black Watch

Private Walter Ernest Howard S. Lancashire Reg.

Private Roland Ivor Tanner 16th Aust. Imp. Fce.

Private Frank Curtis Webb 1st Royal Dragoons, Killed, 21 March 1918, France.

April 1917

Gunner Harold Tucker Phillips Roy. Field Artillery

Private Graham Tucker Hollis 1/4 Dorsetshire R.

May 1917

Sapper Ernest Thompson Royal Engineers

Private Reginald John Fortune Duke of Cornwall's L.I.

Private James Mackinnon 7th Dragoon Guards

June 1917

Private Vernon Henry St.John Viscount Bolingbroke, 3rd Dorsetshire R.

July 1917

Private Ernest Hatter 1st R. Berkshire R.

October 1917

Seaman Ernest Arthur Baden Trueman R.M.S. Bamillier

Seaman William Harris Heath Royal Navy

April 1918

Private George Hunt 91st R. Warwicks R.

June 1918

Private Arthur Ind Wiltshire Reg.

July 1918

Observer Walter Hughes Royal Air Force

Fig 19 - The Roll of Honour in St Mary's Church, photo by Sheridan Parsons

Hay Lane Roll of Honour

The Chapel at Hay Lane produced its own handwritten Roll of Honour. It contains those who served and those who fell. The Roll of Honour reads:

Roll of Honour - Hay Lane

Name - Regiment

Pte George Sawyers, 1st Wilts, d.13.10.14 Mons

Pte James Tuck, 2nd Wilts

Pte George Eacott, 1st Wilts, wounded

Pte Will. Reeves, 2nd Wilts

Pte Fred T Strange 4th R.I. Dragoon Guards

Pte Frank Porter 2nd Wilts, missing June 1915

Bom^{dr} Egbert D Porter, R.F.A. M.M.

Pte Sidney J Porter, 5th Wilts

Pte Will Woodward, 7th Wilts

Pte Harry Woodward, 7th Wilts

Private Sidney Woodward, 7th Wilts

Pte Herbert Waite, R.F.A. India

Drvr. Edward Sawyer, R.F.A. India

Gun Ernest Chard, R.F.A. India

Pte Frank Clifford, R.F.A. India

Pte Joseph Miles, R.F.A. India

Serg' Ernest Townsend, 2nd Wiltshires, d.12.3.15 Neuve Chapelle

Pte Will Fullaway, R.M. Fusiliers, d. 1.9.15 Dardan^elles

Trooper Herbert J Crew, R.W. Yeomanry

Rifln Albert J Strange, 5th Rifle Brigade

Pte Will Bezzant, Wilts A.A.C.

Pte Will Clifford, Wilts d. 19.1.1915 Netley

Trooper Thom. Newman, R. W. Yeomanry

Trooper Alb Sawyers, 12th Hants

Pte Arthur Sawyers, R.F.A.

Pte Alfred Clifford, 6th Wilts

Gun Albert Bezzant, R.F.A. India

Pte Walter Clifford, 4th Wilts, India

Pte Will Newman, 6th Leinster

Pte Victor Lovelock

Pte John Woodward

Gun Harold Phillips, R.F.A.

Pte Graham Hollis, 3rd Dorsets

W H Heath, Royal Navy

Ernest Trueman, Royal Navy

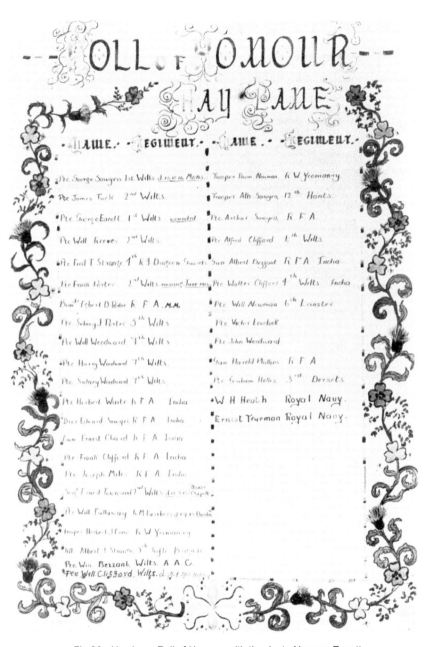

Fig 20 - Hay Lane Roll of Honour, with thanks to Norman Eacott.

Tockenham War Memorial

The Tockenham war memorial at Tockenham Corner includes the names of local men including both those who died and also those who served. It does not give full names, regiments or ranks. The names are inscribed as shown here:

1914 - 1918

H Church - H Fry

P Church - J Hunt

A Church - J Walker

Also Served

G J Buxton - H Painter

T Gough - E Reeves

T Hart - F Skinner

S Hunt - E White

J Benstead - A Yates

Fig 21 - Tockenham War Memorial, photographed by Sheridan Parsons in 2014.

Brinkworth War Memorial and Tablet

The war memorial is situated in Brinkworth Cemetery on the north side of The Street, behind the cemetery railings and just to the right of the cemetery entrance gate. The simple memorial is a tapering pillar of granite on a plinth topped with a small wheel-head cross. A plaque bearing two names was added after WW2. New paving was added around the memorial for the centenary commemorations in 2018. There is also a beautifully carved tablet in St Michael and All Angels Church, Brinkworth. It contains the same names as the war memorial, except that Albert Vines is included.

For God, King, and Country.

To the Glory of God,

and in Grateful Remembrance

of the Twenty Men of this Parish

who Gave their Lives for their

Country in the Great War

1914-1918.

Phillip Carter. Absolom Cutts.

David Edwards. Harry J Eggleton M M.

Ernest V Fry. Christopher Hinton.

Edward Hunt. Harry Hunt.

Robert J Kibble. Alfred W Mapson.

James B Mapson. Sidney E Mapson.

Elton Ody. Frank T Reynolds.

Tom S Stephens. Fred Tanner.

Ernest Vines. Frank Vines.

Sidney Vines. Reginald Wheeler.

Greater Love Hath No Man than This, That a Man

Lay Down his Life for his Friends.

Albert E Vines.[18]

---

[18] Albert E Vines' name is added to the foot of the plinth.

Fig 22 - Brinkworth War Memorial, photo by Sheridan Parsons in 2018

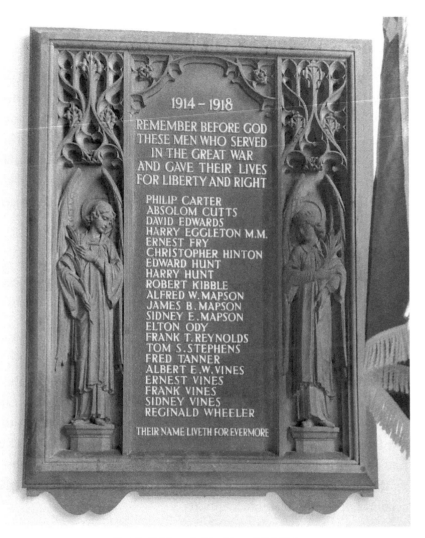

Fig 23 - Brinkworth War Memorial Tablet

Appendixes

Royal Wootton Bassett

Throughout the book, I have referred to the town as Wootton Bassett, rather than Royal Wootton Bassett. The Royal title was not bestowed until the 16th October 2011, for the honour and respect the town showed to members of the Armed Forces during four long years when the repatriations from Lyneham proceeded through the High Street. The Princess Royal delivered the Letters Patent which changed the town's name, granting the prefix on behalf of Her Majesty the Queen, as "an enduring symbol of the nation's admiration and gratitude".

Regimental Numbers

Regimental numbers are given within the body text of the book where known. These are in brackets, immediately after the regiment name, e.g. Royal Army Medical Corps (74794).

Speeches

When reproducing quotes and speeches from original newspapers, I have taken some artistic liberties. The journalistic style of the war years demanded that the majority of public speeches were published in the third person and the past tense. I have restored these speeches to the first person and the present tense as applicable so that they feel closer to the original texts. Naturally, I have relied on the press for the accuracy of the original transcriptions.

CWGC Memorials to the Missing

If you are visiting one of the Commonwealth War Graves Commission memorials to the missing, you may wish to remember these men who have a connection with the Wootton Bassett area.

Arras Memorial

- Hunt, Edward, Private
- Watts, Frank, Lance Corporal
- Webb, Frank Curtis, Private
- Wheeler, Reginald Percy Private

Basra Memorial

- Hughes, Charles Henry, Private
- Mapson, James Benjamin, Private

Helles Memorial

- Comley, John, Private
- Fullaway, William John Thomas, Private

La Ferté-sous-Jouarre Memorial

- White, Eli, Lance Corporal
- Drury, Henry Philip, Private

Le Touret Memorial

- Burchell, William Eli, Private
- Edwards, David, Private
- Hewer, Albert Edward, Private
- Humphries, Frank, Private
- Hunt, Reginald, Private

- Peaple, Albert James, Private
- Sawyer, George Francis, Private
- Stephens, Thomas Stratton, Private
- Townsend, Ernest Arthur, Acting Sergeant

Lone Pine Memorial

- Cox, Ernest Sidney, Private

Loos Memorial

- Gingell, William, Private
- Hinton, Christopher, Private
- Mapson, Sidney Ernest, Private
- Smith, Charles James, Corporal

Menin Gate Memorial

- Angelinetta, Gilbert, Rifleman
- Bridgeman, Montague Roland, Private
- Church, Percy Henry Hardiman, Private
- Hird, John, Private
- Hiscocks, Stanley Albert, Private
- Marsh, Alfred Harry, Private
- Smart, Percy Edward, Private
- Tayler, Harold Lyttleton George, Private
- Twine, Arthur, Private

Ploegsteert Memorial

- Ody, Elton John, Lance Corporal
- Jacobs, William, Private

Pozieres Memorial

- Fry, Ernest Victor, Private
- Walker, Jasper Wilfred, Private
- Titcombe, William, Private
- Cutts, Absalom, Corporal

Thiepval Memorial

- Buckland, Reginald Herbert, Private
- Church, Albert Edward, Private
- Gibbs, Henry James, Lance Corporal
- Gingell, George Henry Lewin, Lance Corporal
- Hunt, Harry John, Private
- Hunt, Lionel Frederick Job, Private, MM
- James, William Henry, Private
- Lovelock, George Edward, Private
- Reeves, Lewis Herbert, Lance Sergeant
- Newman, Reuben Victor, Private
- Sly, William, Sergeant
- Tanner, Fred, Private
- Twine, Arthur Sidney, Private
- Vines, Frank Charles, Private

Tyne Cot Memorial

- Brown, Eltham Bryan, Private
- Lovelock, Victor Rowland, Private
- Broom, William, Private

Vimy Memorial

- Blanchett, Christopher, Sergeant

Vis en Artois Memorial

- Franklin, Leonard, Private

Enlistment

Enlistment is the general process of joining the forces or 'joining up'. The first step for men who volunteered for service was to attest. The would fill out an Attestation Form, with basic details, essentially offering themselves for service. After the introduction of conscription in 1916, men who were conscripted did not attest. They were deemed to have enlisted automatically, therefore, instead of filling out an Attestation Form, they filled out an Enrolment Form.

Men did not always serve immediately on attestation or enrolment. They might be sent home for months, before being called up, or they might be posted immediately to a depot or battalion. Age, marriage, and fitness class, were among the factors which determined when a man would be called up.

Fitness for Service

Each man was medically examined by a medical board on enlistment, and his class of fitness for service was entered on the relevant form. The grades changed over time.

Beginning of the War:

- General Service
- Field service at home
- Garrison service abroad
- Garrison service at home
- Labour
- Sedentary work (cook, clerk, stores, batman etc.)

From May 1916:

- A: General Service
- B1: Abroad; Garrison service
- B2: Labour
- B3: Sedentary work
- C1: At home; Garrison service
- C2: Labour
- C3: Sedentary work

From 1st July 1916:

- A: able to march, see to shoot, hear well and stand active service conditions
- A1: fit for dispatching overseas, as regards physical and mental health and training
- A2: as A1, except for training
- A3: returned Expeditionary Force men, ready except for physical condition
- A4: under 19 who would be A1 or A2 when aged 19
- B: free from serious organic diseases, able to stand service on Lines of Communication, or in garrisons in the tropics
- B1: able to march five miles, see to shoot with glasses and hear well
- B2: able to walk five miles, see and hear sufficiently for ordinary purposes
- B3: only suitable for sedentary work

- C: free from serious organic diseases, able to stand service in garrisons at home

- C1: able to march five miles, see to shoot with glasses and hear well

- C2: able to walk five miles, see and hear sufficiently for ordinary purposes

- C3: only suitable for sedentary work

- D: unfit but likely to become fit within six months

- D1: Regular RA, RE, infantry in Command Depots

- D2: Regular RA, RE, infantry in Regimental Depots

- D3: in any Depot or unit awaiting treatment

- E: unfit and unlikely to become fit within 6 months

Army Ranks

In descending order of rank:

General Officers

Field Marshal: a rank bestowed upon a few senior army officers. (Two crossed batons in a wreath, crown above).

General: the highest level commander, acting in place of the King. (Crossed sword and baton, crown and star above).

Lieutenant-General: acting in place of the General, effectively running the army. (Crossed sword and baton, crown above).

Major General: the army's chief administrative officer dealing with supply, organization, and forming the army for battle or large scale troop movements. (Crossed sword and baton, star above).

Brigadier or Brigadier-General: Commander of a Brigade, a group of three or more Regiments. (Crossed sword and baton).

Field Officers

Colonel: Commander of a Regiment. (Crown above two stars).

Lieutenant-Colonel: the Colonel's assistant, he sometimes commanded his own Battalion. (Crown above one star).

Major: third in command to the Colonel, he sometimes commanded his own Battalion. (Crown).

Company Officers

Captain: head of a company of up to about 200 men, leading them in battle. (Three stars).

Lieutenant: normally leading a small tactical unit such as a platoon. (Two stars).

Second Lieutenant: the Lieutenant's assistant. (One star).

Warrant Officers

Class One: The most senior soldier rank, including Regimental Sergeant Majors, always experienced soldiers, often specialists in their field. A WO1 may act as a senior adviser to a Colonel. (Royal Coat of Arms).

Class Two: a senior management role, including Company Sergeant Majors, focussing on training, welfare and discipline of up to 120 soldiers. A WO2 may act as a senior adviser to a Major. (Crown).

Senior Non-Commissioned Officers

Staff Sergeant: a senior role combining man and resource management of around 120 soldiers, or command of a troop or platoon. (Three stripes and a crown).

Sergeant: typically second in command of a troop or platoon of up to 35 soldiers, and has responsibility for advising and assisting junior officers. (Three stripes).

Junior Non-Commissioned Officers

Corporal: usually experienced soldiers, given command of a group of soldiers, and associated equipment such as tanks and guns. (Two stripes).

Lance Corporal: may supervise a small team of up to four soldiers called a section. (One stripe).

Private: all new soldiers start as Privates. Regimental variations on this rank include sappers, gunners etc. (No insignia)

Service Medals and Clasps.

Fig 24 - Pip, Squeak and Wilfred: the 1914-15 Star, British War Medal and Victory Medal.

1914 Star

Known as Pip, or the Mons Star. Awarded to those who had served in France or Belgium between 5th August 1914 and 22nd November 1914 inclusive. The clasp '5th AUG. - 22nd NOV. 1914' shows that the recipient served under fire. All recipients of the Star also received the British War Medal and the Victory Medal.

The 1914-15 Star

Also known as Pip. Awarded to those who had received the British War Medal, and the Victory Medal who had served in any theatre of war against Germany between 5th August 1914 and 31st December

1915. All recipients of the Star also received the British War Medal and the Victory Medal.

British War Medal

Known as Squeak. Awarded to those who served overseas, whether or not in a theatre of war, between 5th August 1914 and 11th November 1918 inclusive. This was later extended to include service in some areas in 1919 and 1920. Those engaged solely on home service did not qualify.

Victory Medal

Colloquially known as Wilfred. Awarded to those who served in a theatre of war between 5 August 1914 and 11 November 1918. Those engaged solely on home service did not qualify.

Territorial Force War Medal, 1914-1919

Awarded to those who served in a Territorial Force on or before 30th September 1914 and went on to serve in a foreign theatre of war between 5th August 1914 and 11th November 1918. Not awarded to those eligible to receive the 1914 Star or 1914/15.

Silver War Badge

Awarded to those who were discharged or retired from the forces as a result of sickness or injury caused by their war service. From April 1918 this included civilians serving with the Royal Army Medical Corps, female nurses, staff, and aid workers.

Clasp

Clasps are added to a medal for a particular campaign. In the Great War, the most commonly awarded clasp was for those who served under enemy fire during the first sixteen weeks of the war, including the battle of Mons, the retreat to the Seine, the battles of Le Cateau, the Marne, the Aisne and the first battle of Ypres. Approximately five in every twelve medals issued included a clasp. The clasp consists of narrow horizontal bronze stripe sewn onto the ribbon, bearing the dates: 5th AUG - 22nd NOV 1914. Recipients wearing a ribbon rather than a full medal were entitled to attach a small silver heraldic rose to the ribbon.

Gallantry Medals

VC: Victoria Cross. The highest award for gallantry. Awarded to any rank for an act of outstanding courage or devotion to duty in the presence of the enemy.

DSO: Distinguished Service Order. Awarded for bravery to commissioned officers.

DSC: Distinguished Service Cross. Awarded to naval officers below Lieutenant Commander for gallantry at sea in the presence of the enemy.

MC: Military Cross. Awarded to Officers for exemplary gallantry in operations against the enemy on land.

DFC: Distinguished Flying Cross. Awarded to officers and warrant officers for valour, courage or devotion to duty while flying on active operations against the enemy.

AFC: Air Force Cross. Awarded for valour, courage or devotion to duty whilst flying, not in operations against the enemy.

DCM: Distinguished Conduct Medal. Awarded to all other ranks for exceptional bravery.

CGM: Conspicuous Gallantry Medal. Naval equivalent to the DCM.

DSM: Distinguished Service Medal. Naval equivalent to the MM.

MM: Military Medal. Awarded to warrant officers, NCOs and other ranks for gallantry in action against the enemy.

DFM: Distinguished Flying Medal. Royal Air Force equivalent to the MM.

AFM: Air Force Medal. Awarded to British and Commonwealth Forces for valour, courage or devotion to duty whilst flying, but not against the enemy. Equivalent to the MM.

MSM: Meritorious Service Medal. Awarded to all forces for meritorious service or gallantry. Some variations apply.

MID: Mentioned in Despatches.

Citation for a Gallantry Award.

The Gazette

The term 'Gazetted' is used frequently in this book. It refers to the publication of an event in the London Gazette, the Edinburgh Gazette, or the Dublin Gazette, the first official journals of record and the newspaper of the Crown. The Gazette is the bearer of official War Office news such as a promotion or an award for gallantry. The Gazette coined its own terminology for those appearing in its pages. A man was said to have been 'Gazetted' not when the promotion or award occurred, but when his name was published.

The Last Day

I have collected together here the names and burial locations of the nine men who served in the Wiltshire Regiment and died on the last day of the war, 11th November 1918. None were from Wootton Bassett.

Captain Charles Frederic Aubrey Anderson Hooper, age 46, Hartlepool West View Cemetery.

Private W Clements, age 33, St Mary Churchyard, Wheatley.

Corporal Alfred C Stratton, age 30, Southampton Old Cemetery.

Private Thomas H Floyd, Caudry British Cemetery.

Private Lenard Clifton Brock, age 24, Cologne Southern Cemetery.

Private A W Jennings, Cologne Southern Cemetery.

Private A Taylor, age 19, St Joseph's Roman Catholic Cemetery, Moston.

Private C W Frost, age 40, St Sever Cemetery Extension, Rouen.

Private Raymond Cecil Morgan, age 19, St Sever Cemetery Extension, Rouen.

Index of Last Names

Index of Last Names

Lightning Source UK Ltd.
Milton Keynes UK
UKHW011356150819
348014UK00006B/213/P